Rethinking Student Belonging in Higher Education

Arguing for an understanding of belonging in higher education as relational, complex and negotiated, particularly in reference to non-traditional students, *Rethinking Student Belonging in Higher Education* counters prevailing assumptions for what it means to belong and how institutional policy is shaped and implemented around traditional students.

Bringing theoretical insights into institutional areas of policy and practice, this book

- considers what it means to belong as a non-traditional student in a higher education environment designed for traditional students;
- presents the argument for belonging in line with theoretical insights of Bourdieu, Brah and Massey;
- illustrates belonging through case studies drawn from empirical research; and
- presents the argument for a borderland analysis of belonging in higher education, identifying key features and advantages of this theoretical framework.

Reframing belonging within a neo-liberal, marketised higher education sector, *Rethinking Student Belonging in Higher Education* is a topical and accessible point of reference for any academic in the field of higher education policy and practice, as well as those involved in ensuring widening participation, equality, diversity, inclusion and fair access.

Kate Carruthers Thomas is a Senior Research Fellow at Birmingham City University, UK.

Rethinking Student Belonging in Higher Education

From Bourdieu to Borderlands

Kate Carruthers Thomas

Routledge
Taylor & Francis Group

LONDON AND NEW YORK

First published 2019
by Routledge
2 Park Square, Milton Park, Abingdon, Oxon OX14 4RN

and by Routledge
605 Third Avenue, New York, NY 10017

First issued in paperback 2022

Routledge is an imprint of the Taylor & Francis Group, an informa business

Publisher's Note
The publisher has gone to great lengths to ensure the quality of this
reprint but points out that some imperfections in the original copies may
be apparent.

British Library Cataloguing-in-Publication Data
A catalogue record for this book is available from the British Library

Library of Congress Cataloging-in-Publication Data
A catalog record for this book has been requested

ISBN: 978-1-03-240175-1 (pbk)
ISBN: 978-1-138-31137-4 (hbk)
ISBN: 978-0-429-45890-3 (ebk)

DOI: 10.4324/9780429458903

Typeset in Times New Roman
by Apex CoVantage, LLC

This book is dedicated to Professor Sue Jackson, Professor Emeritus, Birkbeck, University of London, without whom this journey would not have begun.

Contents

List of abbreviations   ix

Prologue   1

1 Who belongs in higher education?   9

2 The part-time landscape   19

3 A journey into border territory   25

4 Borderlands and belonging   31

5 Thinking spatially   47

6 A simultaneity of stories-so-far   57

Epilogue   81

Index   85

Abbreviations

ELQ	Equivalent or Lower Qualification
GCE	General Certificate of Education
HE	Higher Education
HEA	Higher Education Academy
HEFCE	Higher Education Funding Council for England
HESA	Higher Education Statistical Agency
NSS	National Student Survey
OFFA	Office for Fair Access
UCAS	Universities and Colleges Admissions Service

Prologue

The function of a prologue is to consider earlier stories pertinent to the plot. This book draws on the process and findings of my doctoral research project: *Dimensions of Belonging: Rethinking Retention for Mature Part-time Undergraduates in English Higher Education* (Thomas 2016). The project was the result of a successful bid by Birkbeck, University of London for external funding from the Higher Education Academy (HEA) Mike Baker Doctoral Programme (2012–2015). The intended topic – the impact of institutional retention strategies on mature part-time undergraduates – was justified by a dearth of pertinent literature and a continuing and significant disparity between rates of full and part-time student retention.

As a researcher, I begin with a map, of sorts: a research topic, working title and a timescale.

This map gives order to the task ahead. It helps me to orientate myself, to select and engage with the literature, to plan fieldwork. The map suggests the boundaries of the research terrain and a potential route through. 'A map tells of an order in things. With the map we can locate ourselves and find our way . . . we map things out to get a feeling for their structure' (Massey 2005, p. 106).

The map is an appealing metaphor, transferable to a variety of contexts and processes. It is also problematic:

> because of the double-sided characteristic of all maps . . . maps are taken to be 'true' and 'objective' measures of the world, and are accorded a kind of benign neutrality . . . the other side of this analogous characteristic is the inevitable abstractness of maps, the result of selection, omission, isolation, distance and codification.
>
> (Corner 1999, pp. 214–215)

The dominant form of mapping (think of a Tube map, a road map, a world map . . .) provides a view from above, purportedly neutral, reducing complexity to an abstraction. Maps give authority to simplified, selective and bounded representations of space, and 'position the observer, themselves unobserved, outside and above the object of the gaze' (Massey 2005, p. 107). A researcher working in the positivist tradition understands research in a similar way: as an objective, neutral activity seeking a truth, unaffected by the positioning and actions of the researcher.

This is not my understanding of research.

Research selects and constructs and involves relationships of power between the researcher and the researched. Process and claims are codified in accordance with academic and disciplinary conventions and furthermore:

> the gendered, multiculturally situated researcher approaches the world with a set of ideas, a framework (theory, ontology) that specifies a set of questions (epistemology) that he or she then examines in specific ways (methodology, analysis).
>
> (Denzin and Lincoln 2008, p. 28)

What if, instead, we see research – and the map – as 'a serious fiction that represents a particular intellectual landscape from a particular point of view' (Gregory 1994, p. 6), as expressions of powerful views of the world, constructed by a mapmaker? As a schoolchild in 1970s' England, my understanding of 'the world' was indisputably shaped by the map on my classroom wall, the ubiquitous Mercator Projection, created by a Flemish expert at the top of his game, using the most advanced technology available to him. Sixteenth-century nautical cartographer Gerardus Mercator addressed the impossibility of presenting a three-dimensional shape on a two-dimensional surface by keeping parallels and meridians as straight lines. In doing so, his map of 'the world' represents countries closer to the Equator as smaller than those farther away, meaning Africa appears smaller than Greenland and the size of Northern Hemisphere European countries is exaggerated. The Mercator projection, so revolutionary in its time 'imparts political authority to a flawed Eurocentric representation of space, one with significant political resonance across centuries' (Carruthers Thomas 2017). The Mercator Projection is now discredited for its bias.

My completed thesis departed somewhat from its original topic and, through a multiple case study of four English universities, re-imagined dominant narratives of belonging and retention in contemporary English HE in relation to mature part-time undergraduates. In that thesis and in this book, I challenge a powerful and ubiquitous narrative of student belonging in HE, a narrative widely referenced across an increasingly managerial, audited and competitive sector and tightly entangled in prevailing agendas of student retention, student engagement and the student experience.

Why belonging? Maslow places belonging after physiological and safety and before esteem and self-actualisation in his hierarchy of needs (1943, 1954). 'A sense of belonging is . . . a basic human need and motivation, sufficient to influence behaviour' (Strayhorn 2012, p. 3). In the context of contemporary HE, belonging is also linked to experiences of mattering or feeling cared about and accepted (Strayhorn 2012; O'Keeffe 2013). So belonging is social:

> a process of creating a sense of identification with, or connection to, cultures, people, places and material objects . . . one of the ways in connections between self and society manifest.
>
> (May 2013, p. 1)

If belonging is social, it is relational: 'Who can achieve belonging and where is always tied to issues of power and inequalities . . . within society' (*ibid.*, p. 154). In the UK, a particular narrative of student belonging is considered critical to retention and success (Thomas 2012). This narrative is ubiquitous, largely uncontested and embedded in the lexicon of institutional strategy, literature and national student agendas. Yet relationships of power and inequality in the sector determine 'who belongs' and 'belonging' is not equally available to all.

I have worked in the HE sector in England since 1999. Between 2002 and 2012 I was employed as a widening participation practitioner and project manager at two different universities, one a research-intensive Russell Group institution, the other a post-1992 'new' university. My work was largely concerned with opening routes into higher education to under-represented groups: young people in lower socio-economic groups, vocational learners, mature students and disabled adult learners. These were boom years for widening participation. The Labour government of 1997 to 2010 funded two major national initiatives in England: Aimhigher and Lifelong Learning Networks, to work towards its stated target of a 50% participation rate for 18- to 30-year-olds (Lupton and Obolenskaya 2013, p. 15). The government also provided a funding premium for UK universities based on their success in recruiting students from lower socio-economic groups.

The longer I worked in widening participation, the more interested I became in these diverse students' experiences of HE and how it varied from 'the norm'. I conducted several small-scale practitioner enquiries into transition and student identity for undergraduates studying in my university's multiple partner colleges (Thomas 2008, 2011). 'Belonging in HE' was not straightforward for these students. Their lives were complex entanglements of locality, employment and family commitments which not only inhibited their capacity to participate in 'typical' student activities but also frequently limited the relevance of such activities to their everyday lives and learning aspirations.

> If you have to think about belonging, perhaps you are already outside.
>
> (Probyn 1996, p. 8)

'Belonging in HE' was not straightforward for me either. My older sister and I were the first in our family to study at university, but I 'dropped out' after my first term because I hated the course and the university I had chosen. I started a different course at another university a year later and went on to complete my degree. I began my higher education in an Arts discipline but after graduation, studied Social Sciences part-time with the Open University alongside full-time employment in the publishing and media sectors. Becoming a widening participation practitioner in HE placed me in a professional 'third space between professional and academic domains . . . colonised primarily by *unbounded* and *blended professionals*' (Whitchurch 2008, pp. 385–386, original italics). These university roles are characterised by flatter management structures, cross-institutional working and 'non-positional authority' (*ibid.*), in other words, responsibility without much power. With hindsight, I suspect the 'unboundedness' of this role may have reinforced an orientation towards future academic interdisciplinarity. During this period, I completed a master's in Education (part-time, also with the Open University).

Belonging is complex in a personal sense for me too. Certain attributes position me in a privileged social position in contemporary Britain – Western, White, British, first-generation middle-class, highly educated – while others – female, gay, childfree – position me more awkwardly in a heteronormative, patriarchal culture.

> Identity can be defined as much by what we are *not* as by who we *are* . . . it is impossible . . . to think through how people can have an identity, that is, be defined by shared characteristics, without working out who is thus excluded – how identity is founded on differentiation.
>
> (Crang 1998, p. 61, original italics)

In my own experience, 'belonging' is neither uniform nor universal. I am more familiar with moving between 'multiple points of attachment, sites of belonging which are not necessarily coterminous with sites of residence' (Schimel 1997, p. 172). Intellectually, personally, viscerally I know it is possible to negotiate meaningful versions of belonging on the periphery, but often these remain invisible to the mainstream and unacknowledged by the centre.

Redundancy, serendipity and uncharacteristic optimism propelled me into full-time doctoral study in my late 40s.

My professional and personal experiences shaped a desire to bring 'into the centre that which has been marginalised . . . telling stories of the silenced, the textually disenfranchised' (Richardson 1997, p. 58). The Phase 1 findings of a national student retention and success change programme, *What Works?* (2008–2011) were highly influential at that time and linked students' 'sense of belonging' to their retention and success (Thomas 2012). In fact, it was impossible to avoid references to belonging when studying the literature of student retention, and it then became impossible for me not to critically engage with the narrative of 'belonging in HE'. I was strongly encouraged to do so by following Bourdieu's sociological framework of analysis. For good reason – Bourdieusian analyses are widely modelled in investigations of unequal educational chances, differential experiences and stratification of the UK HE sector (Reay, Davies, David and Ball 2001; Reay, Crozier and Clayton 2009; Thomas 2002; Bathmaker and Thomas 2009; Abrahams and Ingram 2013; Bathmaker 2015; Waller, Ingram and Ward 2017 *inter alia*). And yet,

> [s]o much is reproduced by the requirement to follow. In the academy you might be asked to follow the well-trodden paths . . . to cite those deemed to have already the most influence. The more a path is used the more a path is used. . . . To deviate from that path can be hard.
>
> (Ahmed 2018)

My thinking and thus my research into mature part-time undergraduates and belonging became influenced by an understanding of belonging as inherently geographical,

> connecting matter to place through various practices of boundary making and inhabitation . . . the need for 'a thorough theorisation of belonging and . . . the differences between a sense of belonging, practices of belonging and formal structures of belonging'.
>
> (Mee and Wright 2009, pp. 772–774)

The well-trodden Bourdieusian path led me some of the way towards a rethinking of belonging, but I began to search for a more nuanced theoretical trajectory, one directed towards an understanding of belonging as relational and complex. In doing so, I deviated from that familiar path and reached an analysis of belonging in which difference is defined, articulated and experienced through relationships of power in space.

This book is a serious fiction.

In it, I map student belonging from my own perspective and my interpretation of others'. As an account, it is 'partial, local and situational . . . our self is always present, no matter how much we try to suppress it' (Richardson 1997, p. 91). The book tells my story of rethinking student belonging, of a theoretical trajectory from Bourdieu to borderlands. It scrutinises practices of belonging and geographies of power on campus and across the sector, intending to provide an analysis transferable to different HE contexts, settings and student constituencies.

My own project is but one point of exchange, one example of multiple criss-crossing, but I hope that my observations come to the surface, leaving traces on the outside that may encourage other movements, hopes of becoming and alternative belongings.

(Probyn 1996, p. 15)

References

Abrahams, J. and Ingram, N., 2013. The chameleon habitus: Exploring local students' negotiation of multiple fields. *Sociological Research Online*, 18 (4), 21.

Ahmed, S., 2018. *Refusal, resignation and complaint* [online]. Available from: https://feministkilljoys.com/2018/06/28/refusal-resignation-and-complaint/ [Accessed 24 July 2018].

Bathmaker, A., 2015. Thinking with Bourdieu: Thinking after Bourdieu. Using 'field' to consider in/equalities in the changing field of English higher education. *Cambridge Journal of Education*, 45 (1), 61–80.

Bathmaker, A. and Thomas, W., 2009. Positioning themselves: An exploration of the nature and meaning of transitions in the context of dual sector FE/HE institutions in England. *Journal of Further and Higher Education*, 33 (2), 119–130.

Carruthers Thomas, K., 2017. Towards a methodology: Organisational cartographies. *International Journal of Professional Management: Special Edition: Arts and Management*, 12 (3), 55–64.

Corner, J., 1999. The agency of mapping: Speculation, critique and invention. *In*: Cosgrove, D., ed. *Mappings*. London: Reaktion, 213–252.

Crang, M., 1998. *Cultural geography*. London: Routledge.

Denzin, N. and Lincoln, Y., 2008. *Strategies of qualitative inquiry*. 3rd ed. Thousand Oaks: Sage.

Gregory, D., 1994. *Geographical imaginations*. Oxford: Basil Blackwell.

Lupton, R. and Obolenskaya, P., 2013. *Labour's record on education: Policy, spending and outcomes 1997–2010*. Social Policy in a Cold Climate Working Paper 3. London: Centre for Analysis of Social Exclusion, LSE.

Maslow, A.H., 1943. A theory of human motivation. *Psychological Review*, 50 (4), 370–396.

Maslow, A.H., 1954. *Motivation and personality*. New York, NY: Harper.

Massey, D., 2005. *For space*. London: Sage.

May, V., 2013. *Connecting self to society: Belonging in a changing world*. London: Palgrave Macmillan.

Mee, K. and Wright, S., 2009. Geographies of belonging. *Environment and Planning A*, 41, 772–779.

O'Keeffe, P., 2013. A sense of belonging: Improving student retention. *College Student Journal*, 47 (4), 606–613.

Probyn, E., 1996. *Outside belongings*. New York and London: Routledge.

Reay, D., Crozier, G. and Clayton, J., 2009. Strangers in paradise? Working-class students in elite universities. *Sociology*, 43 (6), 1103–1121.

Reay, D., Davies, J., David, M. and Ball, S., 2001. Choices of degree or degrees of choice? Class, 'race' and the higher education choice process. *Sociology*, 35 (4), 855–874.

Richardson, L., 1997. *Fields of play: Constructing an academic life*. New Brunswick, NJ: Rutgers University Press.

Schimel, L., 1997. Diaspora, sweet diaspora: Queer culture to post-Zionist Jewish identity. *In*: Queen, C. and Schimel, L., eds. *PoMoSexuals: Challenging assumptions about gender and sexuality*. San Francisco, CA: Cleiss Press, 163–173.

Strayhorn, T.L., 2012. *College students' sense of belonging: A key to educational success for all students*. New York: Routledge.

Thomas, K., 2008. *Part of the bigger picture*. Bristol: University of the West of England.

Thomas, K., 2011. *Working on transition*. Bristol: University of the West of England.

Thomas, K., 2016. *Dimensions of belonging: Rethinking retention for mature part-time undergraduates in English higher education* (PhD). Birkbeck, University of London, London, UK.

Thomas, L., 2002. Student retention in higher education: The role of institutional habitus. *Journal of Education Policy*, 17 (4), 423–442.

Thomas, L., 2012. *Engagement and belonging in higher education in a time of change: A summary of findings and recommendations from the what works? Student retention & success programme*. Executive Summary. Bristol: HEFCE.

Waller, R., Ingram, N. and Ward, M.R.M., 2017. *Higher education and social inequalities: Getting in, getting on, getting out*. London: Routledge.

Whitchurch, C., 2008. Shifting identities and blurring boundaries: The emergence of third space professionals in UK higher education. *Higher Education Quarterly*, 62 (4), 377–396.

1   Who belongs in higher education?

Introduction

> At the heart of successful retention and success is a strong sense of belonging in HE for all students. This is most effectively nurtured through mainstream activities that all students participate in.
>
> – Thomas (2012, p. 6)

This statement summarises the prevailing understanding of student belonging in the UK HE sector. It embeds belonging within an array of national student agendas and positions it 'at the heart' of student retention, that is 'the extent to which learners remain within a higher education institution, and complete a programme of study in a pre-determined time-period' (Jones 2008, p. 1). This understanding of belonging is central to the *What Works?* student retention and success change programme (2008–2017), a national evidence-based initiative 'focused on identifying and implementing whole-institutional approaches to improving student retention and success' (HEA 2018). The initiative was funded by the Paul Hamlyn Foundation and delivered in partnership by the HEA and Action on Access.

This chapter looks closely at this influential narrative. It places it within historical and contemporary contexts; tracing the continuing influence of Tinto's US model of student persistence (1975) and the adaptation of interactional experiences of congruency and integration to student belonging in a UK context. The chapter problematises the narrative, highlighting the way in which an emphasis on mainstream practices and conformity 'promoting tacit assumptions that a typical HE student is full-time, young, time-rich and at least initially, resident on or near campus' (Thomas 2015, p. 38). This simultaneously positions in deficit those whose characteristics and modes of engagement with university study differ from that norm.

Belonging in the changing spaces of higher education

The *What Works?* programme was one in a line of responses to continuing concerns about student retention which emerged following moves towards the massification of UK HE. When Robbins's Committee on Higher Education first convened in 1961, the territory of English HE was limited and tightly guarded. Eight per cent of school leavers went on to HE, attending one of 24 universities. Three out of 20 attended Oxford or Cambridge; 'academic leaders and political and administrative leaders were all members of the same national elite. They shared the same silent allegiance to the same unarticulated values' (Scott 1998, p. 45). The Robbins Principle, that 'courses of higher education should be available for all who are qualified by ability and attainment to pursue them and wish to do so' (Robbins 1963), implied that a wider section of the population rightfully belonged in HE and that the sector should adapt accordingly. The expansion of HE's physical and socio-economic spaces involved the conversion of Advanced Colleges of Technology into technological universities, the creation of new 'plate-glass universities' and polytechnics and the launch of the Open University. These developments transformed the UK HE sector from 24 universities only accessible to a national elite (Scott 1998) to a landscape of multiple higher education providers serving a significantly larger and more diverse student body. The announcement of a 'binary divide' in Antony Crosland's Woolwich Polytechnic Speech of 1965 (Hillman 2016) led to the transformation of over 50 existing technical and large regional colleges into 30 polytechnics between 1969 and 1972. These were the primary engines for growth in the system, bringing 'students with a wider range of backgrounds, achievements and experiences into English higher education especially adults holding non-traditional qualifications' (Parry 2006, p. 397). Their students became part of the university sector when the 1988 Education Reform Act removed polytechnics from local authority control and granted them membership of the university 'club'.

Yet Trow argues that the UK sector's growth was limited by the existing elite model, 'affirming values and assumptions that define the English "idea of a university" . . . incompatible with the provision of mass higher education' (Trow 1989, p. 56). The UK HE system became sharply stratified: 'one layer consisting of a high qualification on entry, limited low participation neighbourhoods' students and long standing university charter group . . . the second layer with the obverse attributes' (Longden 2013, p. 142). The 'old' pre-1992 universities retained their selective nature in contrast to the more active recruitment practised by 'new' post-1992 institutions. Combined with the more vocational and applied nature of the programmes offered by the latter, this maintained the pre-1992 universities as the territory of the traditional middle-class full-time student and corralled the majority of non-traditional students, including mature part-time undergraduates, into post-1992 universities. The binary divide had been replaced with a newly badged line of division running between pre- and post-1992 universities, with implications for those who studied either side.

Overall participation in HE increased from 8.4% in 1970, to 19.3% in 1990 and to 33% in 2000 (Bolton 2012, p. 14). The sector's rapid expansion throughout the 1980s and 1990s raised concerns about the suitability of new student constituencies to participate in it and about resourcing and value for public money as articulated in the Secretary of State for Education and Employment's annual letter to the HEFCE: 'widening access to higher education must not lead to an increase in the number of people who fail to complete their courses' (Blunkett 2000). The National Audit Office (2002) also highlighted the challenge of widening participation and the importance of 'bearing down on non-completion'. The student retention agenda was 'managerially oriented, signalling a focus on the effectiveness and efficiency of an institution or a system' (Yorke and Longden 2004, p. 5). Two large-scale autopsy studies (Yorke 1999; Davies and Elias 2002), both heavily weighted towards young, full-time undergraduates, identified multiple reasons for students leaving HE, including flawed decision-making about programme choice, students' experience of the programme and the institution, failure to cope with demands of the programme and events that impacted on students' lives outside the institution (Yorke and Longden 2004, p. 141).

A decade later, in a significantly more marketised and metricised system, Rose-Adams's (2012) research into student withdrawal returned broadly similar findings, highlighting institutional and course match, academic experience, and problems with social integration as principal reasons for leaving university. He also notes that while there are often multiple reasons for leaving HE, the reason given tends to be the one dominant for the student at that point in time. An institution-centric understanding of student retention 'generally conceived . . . with a focus on the "economic" variables of time and measurable outcomes' (Hewitt and Rose-Adams 2013, p. 147) is at odds with such plurality and 'insufficient to create truly meaningful understanding of successful individual learning journeys and experiences' (*ibid.*, p. 143).

Since 2010, the increasing exposure of UK HE to market forces and the switch to a funding system relying primarily on fees paid by students (through loans provided by the government) have markedly increased retention's significance to an institution's reputational and economic health. Any students who leave before completing their course not only 'wastes the resources that were committed to recruiting and enrolling them' (Yorke and Longden 2004, p. 9); they also present a risk to the university's league table rankings and represent lost institutional income in the form of tuition fees, and associated costs such as residential fees.

Pre-1992 universities have retention rates at the higher end of the spectrum while students in post-1992 universities are structurally more vulnerable to withdrawal as these institutions are more likely to attract and accept non-traditional learners with lower entry qualifications, including those without recent GCE A Levels.

What Works?

The *What Works?* programme (Thomas 2012; Thomas, Hill, O'Mahoney and Yorke 2017) broke new ground in moving the focus away from the individual student and towards universities' obligations to their students. Greater significance was placed on an interpretation of retention as a 'complex social process of student-institution negotiation' (Ozga and Sukhnandan 1998, p. 316). *What Works?* recommendations are framed by three proposals: that it is crucial to address student retention within institutional strategy and policy, that having admitted a student an institution has an ethical obligation to take reasonable steps to enable them to be successful and that institutional retention strategy should be mainstreamed rather than aimed at specific groups (2012, p. 4). These proposals imply an acknowledgement of 'institutional habitus', the extension of the Bourdieusian concept of habitus to organisations (McDonough 1996; Reay, David and Ball 2001; Thomas 2002). 'Educational institutions favour knowledge and experiences of dominant social groups . . . to the detriment of other groups' (Thomas 2002, p. 431), but 'if an institution is accepting and celebratory of difference, students from diverse backgrounds will see themselves better reflected in the institution and be more likely to persist' (*ibid.*, p. 439).

What Works? invested considerable effort into developing and communicating an evidence base for retention and success across the UK sector. Phase 1 involved 22 English higher education providers in a three-year research programme and Phase 2 a further 13 in extended implementation and evaluation. The Phase 1 meta-analysis and final report, aimed at UK university leaders (Thomas 2012), emphasises an institutional obligation to 'nurture a sense of belonging' in order to maximise student retention and success' (*ibid.*, p. 70). The notion of student belonging in HE is associated with particular kinds of 'student' behaviour enacted within campus boundaries and/or outside contact hours: 'our definition of belonging is closely aligned with the concept of student engagement, encompassing both academic and social' (*ibid.*, p. 6). Living at home, combining study with employment, and entering HE later are identified as ways of engaging which 'make it more difficult for students to fully participate, integrate and feel like they belong in HE, which can impact on their retention and success' (*ibid.*). This is problematic in three key ways. First, it privileges mainstream student identities and behaviours and thus promotes a narrow and reductive understanding of student belonging; second, it reinforces that privilege and positions 'other' student identities in deficit by outlining a set of problematic behaviours which place 'belonging' at risk; and, third, it makes a direct association between this version of 'belonging' and student retention. It is an approach which clearly shows the influence of US student retention literature and of one model in particular.

Tinto's model: integration and congruency

It is difficult to overstate the influence of Tinto's paradigmatic model of student departure (1975) on the UK narrative of student belonging. Tinto sought to formulate 'a theoretical model that explains the processes of interaction between the individual and the institution that leads differing individuals to drop out from institutions of higher education' (*ibid.*, p. 90). Tinto argues that psychological theories of student departure which emphasise individual abilities offer only 'a partial truth' and 'ignore the fact that individual departure is a function of the environment in which individuals find themselves' (*ibid.*, p. 87). Instead, he 'emphasises the requirement for a match between institution and student and for integration in both academic and social spheres' (Thomas 2015).

Groundbreaking in its time, the model built on broader understandings of withdrawal or departure as an absence of integration in a community, that is the extent to which students adapt themselves to the culture of the university.

> The process of educational departure is not substantially different from the other processes of leaving which occur among human communities generally. In both instances, departure mirrors the absence of social and intellectual integration into the mainstream of community life and the social support such integration provides.
>
> (Tinto 1987, p. 180)

Tinto's model draws on van Gennep's study of rites of membership of tribal societies (1960) and Durkheim's study of suicide (1961). Van Gennep's description of the three stages of 'the movement of individuals from membership in one group to that of another . . . separation, transition, incorporation' (Tinto 1987, p. 92) offers a framework for thinking about 'the longitudinal process of student persistence and by extension, the time-dependent process of student departure' (*ibid.*, p. 94). At the start of their university course the individual moves from 'the position of a known member of one group, to that of a stranger in the new setting' (1989, p. 441), and unless transition and incorporation are successfully achieved, this can lead to a state of 'temporary normlessness' and potential withdrawal, which Tinto compares to Durkheim's definition of 'egotistical' suicide. Student persistence is presented as a linear, sequential process in which interruption has a negative impact on the status of the individual and his or her relationship with other members of the community.

For persistence to occur, Tinto argues, new students need to 'become competent members of academic and social communities of the college' (1989, p. 452), although, while academic performance is a 'minimal formal condition for persistence . . . integration in the social system is not' (1987, p. 107). The model combines factors of difficulty, incongruence and isolation with notions of individual disposition, describing the latter as 'the roots of individual departure' (*ibid.*, p. 35). These include background characteristics (socio-economic status, educational background, gender, ethnicity, age) as well as attributes which can affect an individual's potential or ability to integrate with the intellectual and social life of the institution. Tinto categorises these as (a) the dispositions of individuals (intention, commitment) and (b) the nature of the individual's interactional experiences with the institution (adjustment, difficulty, congruence and isolation).

Tinto's model has been internationally influential for over five decades but has not escaped criticism. Herzog questions the adequacy of a model 'steeped in, or derived from, the interactionalist theories of student departure . . . developed over 20 years ago based on academically and socio-economically more homogenous, full-time cohorts' (2005, p. 886). Tanaka challenges Tinto's acceptance of underlying cultural norms of the institution which are embedded within his (pre-existing) survey instruments:

> In retrospect, we now know that Tinto's original conception of integration was handicapped by the surveys – and jargon – of his time. Cultural bias seems embedded in the very name of the theory, 'integration' implying assimilation to dominant norms. Thus, although Tinto's conception might allow researchers to discover how to help American Indian students adjust to a 'mainstream white college environment, it does little to expose and unseat the undemocratic play of power there'.
>
> (Tanaka 2002, p. 273)

Tanaka questions why research methods on college student development have not kept pace with the proliferation of social theory since the 1970s addressing the connection among culture, power and knowledge (*ibid.*,

p. 263). This reflects wider criticism of US retention literature for its reliance 'on causal modelling research most frequently centred on white, middle-class, young American freshers in private residential institutions' (Yorke and Longden 2004, p. 75).

Tinto acknowledges the limitations of the original model in his revisions to it (1986a, 1986b, 1987, 1989). He agreed it reflected a

> lack of sufficient emphasis to the role of finances . . . a failure to highlight differential educational careers that mark the experience of students of different gender, race and social status . . . (and) those forms of disengagement occurring within the two-year college.
>
> (Tinto 1987, p. 689)

He also notes older learners' 'qualitatively different experiences of separation, transition and incorporation from young, traditional students' (*ibid.*, p. 454) and, in later work, focused on experiences of commuting, and 'under-prepared' students in the sector. He concludes that participation in collaborative learning activity 'helps bond students to the broader social communities of the college while also engaging them more fully in the academic life of the institution' (Tinto 1997, p. 613), promoting the feelings that they 'belonged in college' (Engstrom and Tinto 2008, p. 4). However, Tanaka argues that Tinto's continued failure to take account of race, ethnicity and gender means his 'formulation is unable to provide for an examination of issues of voice, power, authenticity and reflexivity or to make reconstitution possible' (Tanaka 2002, p. 273).

Systems of HE in the US and UK are profoundly different. Not only is the US system substantially larger, but it is also decentralised and mostly independent. It has the highest rate of student attrition – between 30% and 50% – in the industrialised world (O'Keeffe 2013, p. 605), whereas the UK has one of the lowest. Ozga and Sukhnandan argue that Tinto's model has limited relevance for use in the British context given that it makes 'assumptions about student conformity and adaptation to the institution' and thus may be 'culturally specific to the US and not transferable to UK systems' (Ozga and Sukhnandan 1998, p. 318). Nevertheless, although partially disguised by different terminology and emphasis, key aspects of Tinto's model have become touchstones in the UK retention literature and institutional strategy. Both US and UK narratives of belonging encompass academic and social spheres, identify the relationship between individual and institution (university) as central and model student belonging on an engagement with HE characterised by full-time study and involvement in extra-curricular involvement in 'clubs, societies, the students' union and shared living arrangements' (Thomas 2012, p. 6). It is implied that such forms of engagement are essential if new students are to 'become competent members of academic and social communities of the college' (Tinto 1989, p. 452). Belonging is positioned as a retention solution. However, the UK HE sector is complex and stratified. Its student population is socio-economically, ethnically and educationally diverse, engaging with higher-level study in multiple ways. A Tinto-esque narrative of congruency and integration fails to acknowledge the ways structural factors of age, gender, ethnicity, class and culture inhibit access to the means of belonging it validates. Moreover, it positions those who are perceived as 'not belonging' as problematic rather than the reductive nature of the narrative itself.

References

Blunkett, D., 2000. *Speech on higher education at Maritime Greenwich University* [online]. Available from: http://cms1.gre.ac.uk/dfee/#speech 2000 [Accessed 13 July 2013].

Bolton, P., 2012 *Education: Historical statistics.* House of Commons Library Standard Note SN/SG/4252 [online]. Available from: http://dera.ioe.ac.uk/22771/1/SN04252.pdf [Accessed 11 November 2018].

Davies, R. and Elias, P., 2002. *Dropping out: A study of early leavers from higher education.* Research Report RR386. Department for Education and Skills. Norwich: HMSO.

Durkheim, E., 1961. *Suicide,* translated by J.A. Spaulding and G. Simpson. Glencoe: The Free Press. Paris: Felix Alcan (1897).

Engstrom, C. and Tinto, V., 2008. *Access without support is not opportunity.* 36th annual institute for chief academic officers, the Council of Independent Colleges, Seattle, 1 November.

HEA, 2018. *What works? Student retention and success programme* [online]. Available from: www.heacademy.ac.uk/individuals/strategic-priorities/retention/what-works [Accessed 2 September 2018].

Herzog, S., 2005. Measuring determinants of student return vs dropout/stopout vs transfer: A first to second year analysis of new freshmen. *Research in Higher Education,* 46 (8), 883–927.

Hewitt, L. and Rose-Adams, J., 2013. What retention means to me: The position of the adult learner in student retention. *Widening Participation and Lifelong Learning,* 14 (Special issue: Winter 2012–2013), 146–164.

Hillman, N., 2016. *Polytechnics or universities* [blog], 1 September. Available from: www.hepi.ac.uk/2016/08/15/polytechnics-or-universities/ [Accessed 2 September 2018].

Jones, R., 2008. *Student retention and success: A synthesis of research.* EvidenceNet. York: HEA.

Longden, B., 2013. 'Bearing down' on student non-completion: Implications and consequences for English higher education. *Journal of College Student Retention,* 14 (1), 117–147.

McDonough, P., 1996. *Choosing colleges: How social class and schools structure opportunity.* New York: State University of New York Press.

National Audit Office, 2002. *Improving student achievement in English higher education.* London: National Audit Office.

O'Keeffe, P., 2013. A sense of belonging: Improving student retention. *College Student Journal*, 47 (4), 606–613.

Ozga, J. and Sukhnandan, L., 1998. Undergraduate non-completion: Developing an explanatory model. *Higher Education Quarterly*, 52 (3), 316–333.

Parry, G., 2006. Policy-participation trajectories in English higher education. *Higher Education Quarterly*, 60 (4), 392–412.

Reay, D., David, M. and Ball, S., 2001. Making a difference? Institutional habituses and higher education choice. *Sociological Research Online*, 5 (4) [online]. Available from: htttp://www.socresonline.org.uk/5/4/reay.html [Accessed 4 March 2013].

Robbins, L., 1963. *Higher education: A report of the committee on higher education under the chairmanship of Lord Robbins 1961–63.* Cmnd 2154. London: Stationery Office.

Rose-Adams, J., 2012. *Leaving university early: A research report from the back on course project.* Milton Keynes: The Open University.

Scott, P., 1998. Blueprint or blue remembered hills? The relevance of the Robbins Report to the present reforms of higher education. *Oxford Review of Education*, 14 (1), 33–48.

Tanaka, G., 2002. Higher education's self-reflexive turn: Toward an intercultural theory of student development. *Journal of Higher Education*, 73 (2), 263–296.

Thomas, K., 2015. Rethinking belonging through Bourdieu, diaspora and the spatial. *Widening Participation and Lifelong Learning*, 17 (1), 37–48.

Thomas, L., 2002. Student retention in higher education: The role of institutional habitus. *Journal of Education Policy*, 17 (4), 423–442.

Thomas, L., 2012. *Engagement and belonging in higher education in a time of change: A summary of findings and recommendations from the what works? Student retention & success programme.* Executive Summary. Bristol: HEFCE.

Thomas, L., Hill, M., O'Mahoney, J. and Yorke, M., 2017. *Supporting student success: Strategies for institutional change.* Full Report. London: Paul Hamlyn Foundation.

Tinto, V., 1975. Dropout from higher education: A theoretical synthesis of recent research. *Review of Education Research*, 45, 89–125.

Tinto, V., 1986a. Limits of theory and practice in student attrition. *Journal of Higher Education*, 53 (6), 687–700.

Tinto, V., 1986b. Theories of student departure revisited. *In*: Smart, J., ed. *Higher education: A handbook of theory and research.* Vol. 2. New York: Agathon, 359–384.

Tinto, V., 1987. *Leaving college: Rethinking the causes and cures of student attrition.* Chicago, IL: University of Chicago Press.

Tinto, V., 1989. Stages of student departure: Reflections on the longitudinal character of student leaving. *Journal of Higher Education*, 59, 438–455.

Tinto, V., 1997. Classrooms as communities: Exploring the educational character of student persistence. *Journal of Higher Education*, 68 (6), 599–623.

18 *Who belongs in higher education?*

Trow, M., 1989. The Robbins trap: British attitudes and the limits of expansion. *Higher Education Quarterly*, 43 (1), 55–75.

Van Gennep, A., 1960. *The rites of passage*, translated by M. Vizedon and G. Caffee. Chicago, IL: University of Chicago Press (1909).

Yorke, M., 1999. *Leaving early: Undergraduate non-completion in higher education*. London: Taylor & Francis.

Yorke, M. and Longden, B., 2004. *Retention and student success in higher education*. Maidenhead: Open University Press.

2 The part-time landscape

Introduction

The research on which this book is based focuses on mature, part-time undergraduates in English HE. The characteristics and experiences of part-time study and students are therefore foregrounded. However, I am arguing for a contemporary theorising of belonging in HE relevant to the complex lives of a diverse student population as a whole. Structural factors, characteristics and attributes overlap and intersect across multiple 'groups' within the student population. This rethinking of student belonging is therefore relevant to students of diverse class and race backgrounds, of all ages, those who commute daily to their university, are student parents and/or carers and/ or engage in paid work while studying.

The demographic profile of the UK student population continues to evolve. Overall levels of participation by 'young' students, that is those under 21 (HESA 2018a) rose to 42% in 2006 and 49% in 2015. The overall number of females participating in HE stood at 57% in 2016/7 (HESA 2018b), with the gender gap widening to 11.9% in favour of females in 2015/6 (Department of Education 2017). In 2016/7 one quarter of full-time, first-degree undergraduates were of Black, Asian and Other ethnicities (HESA 2018a). Just as important, the ways in which students of all ages engage with HE have become more diverse. In 2014/5, '55.8% of young students stayed local for university . . . with students' sensitivity to distance increasing the more disadvantaged they are . . . Pakistani and Bangladeshi girls are particularly likely to stay at a local university' (Donnelly and Gamsu 2018, pp. 4–8). Race, gender and class play an important role in university choice. Staying local is also key to mature part-time undergraduates' university choices.

Part-time study

'In England . . . the most common . . . definition of part-time undergraduate students is negative – it is those who do not fit the definition of full-time students' (Callender 2013, p. 131). Part-time undergraduates are more likely to be female, White and studying in a post-1992 HEI for a sub-degree-level qualification (Callender, Hopkin and Wilkinson 2010; HESA 2018b). The majority (52%) of part-time undergraduates are 30 years and over, 38% are between 21 and 29 years and only 10% are 20 years and under. Of part-time undergraduates, 84% are White, 6% Black, 6% Asian and 4% of Other ethnicity (HESA 2018b). They are 'a heterogeneous group, with a very different set of characteristics, motivations and needs, as compared to their full-time counterparts' (Oxford Economics 2014, p. III).

> Part-time undergraduates are more likely than full-time to have lower or no prior educational qualifications and a majority enter HE without GCE A Level qualifications. However they are also more likely than full-time undergraduates to have higher entry qualifications, including first degrees.
>
> (Thomas 2015, p. 39)

Part-time students embark on an extended relationship with the university alongside multiple personal and professional commitments. Their age and gender profile means that they are markedly more likely than their young full-time peers to have family responsibilities and to be in employment during study (Callender *et al.* 2010). Unlike young, full-time undergraduates who are more likely to fit lower occupational level part-time or seasonal work around their studies, part-time students tend to have existing full-time jobs in higher-level occupations, with a bias towards the public sector (Callender and Wilkinson 2011). The intention of part-time study is often to re- or up-skill, potentially to change or enhance career prospects, and many mature part-time undergraduates fit their studies around their jobs, engaging in 'hybrid forms of participation . . . a two-way navigation between studentship and employment "spaces" as well as along often interrelated studentship and employment trajectories' (Fuller 2007, p. 224).

Part-time study has always been a part of the UK HE system. The Robbins Report (1963) was published when, encouraged by a complex system of advanced further education and evening provision funded by local government, levels of part-time participation in HE closely matched full-time participation. However, Carswell (1988) argues that the Robbins Report was based on two key but tacit assumptions, the first being the idea of full-time degree study over three years:

> the Robbins Committee . . . saw full-time studentship as having primacy and considered it was qualitatively superior to, and distinguishable from, part-time studentship. It . . . underlay many of the costings

and the whole presentation of the proposals which made such a deep impression on the public mind in terms of 'student places'.

(*ibid.*, p. 23)

In addition, by awarding grants to residential university students, the Robbins Report assumed the desirability of leaving home to study at university, something which increased substantially in the middle of the twentieth century (*ibid.*, p. 25). The launch of the Open University in 1969 offered students the possibility of learning in their own home, alongside their regular lives. Trow (1989) argues this 'drained off' demand for face-to-face part-time study in traditional HE settings. Certainly it contributed to making part-time students less visible.

This lack of visibility has continued until recently, alongside a long-term decline in part-time study (Callender and Thompson 2018, p. 3). Policy makers have remained largely, sometimes wilfully indifferent to part-time provision and students. Protracted learning pathways and less mobile graduate trajectories do not fit neatly into the dominant and measured agendas of engagement and employability which drive university league tables. Research on financial returns for part-time study shows that in the long term, 'salaries grow at a slower pace and are more likely to stagnate between six months and three and a half years after graduation compared with their full-time peers' (*ibid.*, p. 55). While they are ostensibly embedded within popular narratives of upward social mobility, their university and post-graduation choices are primarily shaped by the need to remain local for family and employment reasons. 'They are more likely than their full-time peers to make a single application to their local university. This increases the chance of making the wrong choice' (Thomas 2015). Students applying with a single choice or through Clearing are more likely to leave university early (Rose-Adams 2012), and this relates to an additional factor which places them under the spotlight as a problematic group: the significant and stubborn disparity in completion rates between full-time and part-time undergraduates. In 2016/17, non-continuation rates for full-time first-degree students averaged 6.4%, while comparable rates for part-time first-degree students averaged 34.2% (HESA 2018c).

Part-time HE in England is in crisis. A perfect storm of changes to HE funding, rising fees, limited eligibility to funding support, economic recession and greater debt aversion among older learners has carved a bleak contemporary landscape.

The number of part-time undergraduate entrants . . . has fallen annually. Part-time students have attracted significant attention recently because

> part-time HE study is in crisis. By 2015, the numbers nationally had decreased by 51% (43,000). . . . These numbers continue to fall.
>
> (Callender and Thompson 2018, p. 3)

The storm began in 2008 with the introduction of the ELQ ruling, which removed HEFCE funding to English institutions teaching students studying for a qualification equivalent to, or lower than, a qualification they already held. Providers now required Home and European Union students studying for an ELQ to pay the full cost of their tuition.

> The ELQ policy was not specifically targeted at continuing education, lifelong learning or part-time students. Nevertheless the effect was most harshly felt by these constituencies because the greatest numbers of students already holding University qualifications were those studying in later life, often part-time, while working, for career development or diversification.
>
> (Lingwood 2015, p. 78)

Specialist part-time HE providers, the Open University and Birkbeck, University of London, argued that the ruling unfairly targeted the part-time sector. From the date of its introduction, the ELQ ruling was blamed for a dramatic scaling back and closure of public and continuing education programmes across the university sector (Atwood 2009). The Open University and Birkbeck were given a two-year grace period but became subject to the ruling in 2010.

The precipitous decline in part-time HE accelerated due to the 2012 reforms which abolished tuition fee and course grants for part-time undergraduates and introduced loans instead (Callender and Thompson 2018, p. 6). Loans were assumed to be equally appropriate instruments for full and part-time undergraduates because the financial return on higher-level study made them affordable. However, economic recession and employment patterns of older learners means uncertain returns on investment and loan take-up by part-time mature undergraduates has been far lower than by their full-time peers. Part-time students have multiple commitments, are more likely to be debt-averse and are less likely to be eligible for loans. In 2012 only 41% were eligible compared to 94% of full-time undergraduates, and only 59% of those eligible took up loans. Despite recognition that 'the UK relies heavily on part-time higher education to up-skill the population . . . to meet fast changing skills needs in a fast changing world' (Universities UK 2013) and the widespread Part-time Matters campaign which championed the benefits of part-time HE and raised awareness of the challenges it faces, actions to stem the decline in part-time provision and student numbers have been minimal.

Part-time undergraduates are in a precarious position within HE in a strategic sense. They are also peripheral to the university campus. Because part-time study offers an opportunity for those whose work or family responsibilities make full-time study impractical' (*ibid.*, p. 4), mature part-time undergraduates are unlikely to participate in clubs, societies, the students' union and shared living arrangements. Structural factors, age and gender, in particular, therefore restrict their access to the means of belonging recognised and validated in dominant institutional and sector discourses. In the following chapters, I begin to rethink student belonging in HE as a relational, complex process, for students positioned as 'different' or 'other'. The following deceptively simple statement is my starting point: 'belonging . . . is often used in a way that implies a common understanding of what belonging is and why belonging is important. Needless to say, no such common understanding exists' (Mee and Wright 2009, p. 772). I challenge and energise familiar analytical templates and seek new theoretical territory between different perspectives to move towards a contemporary theorising of student belonging compatible with diverse students' lives.

References

Atwood, R., 2009. Lifelong learning threatened by funding change. *Times Higher Education* [online], 12 March. Available from: www.timeshighereducation.com/news/lifelong-learning-threatened-by-funding-change/405768.article [Accessed 30 March 2014].

Callender, C., 2013. Part-time undergraduate student funding and financial support. *In*: Callender, C. and Scott, P., eds. *Browne and beyond: Modernizing English higher education* [online]. Available from: http://eprints.ioe.ac.uk/17608/1/Browne_and_Beyond_1st_proof.pdf [Accessed 4 February 2015].

Callender, C., Hopkin, R. and Wilkinson, D., 2010. *Futuretrack: Part-time students career decision-making and career development of part-time higher education students*. Manchester: HECSU.

Callender, C. and Thompson, J., 2018. *The lost part-timers: The decline of part-time undergraduate higher education in England*. London: Sutton Trust.

Callender, C. and Wilkinson, D., 2011. *The impact of higher education for part-time students*. Evidence Report 36. UKCES [online]. Available from: www.ukces.org.uk/assets/ukces/docs/publications/evidence-report-36-impact-of-he-for-pt-students.pdf [Accessed 8 March 2013].

Carswell, J., 1988. What Robbins took for granted. *Oxford Review of Education*, 14 (1), 21–32.

Committee on Higher Education, 1963. *Higher education: report*. London: HMSO [online]. Available from: http://www.educationengland.org.uk/documents/robbins/ [Accessed 9 November 2018].

Department of Education, 2017. SFR47/2017 [online], 28 September. Available from: https://assets.publishing.service.gov.uk/government/uploads/system/uploads/attachment_data/file/648165/HEIPR_PUBLICATION_2015-16.pdf [Accessed 3 September 2018].

Donnelly, M. and Gamsu, S., 2018. *Home and away: Social, spatial and ethnic inequalities in student mobility.* London: The Sutton Trust.

Fuller, A., 2007. Mid-life 'transitions' to higher education: Developing a multi-level explanation of increasing participation. *Studies in the Education of Adults*, 39 (2), 217–235.

HESA, 2018a. *Definitions and benchmark factors: Age markers* [online]. Available from: www.hesa.ac.uk/data-and-analysis/performance-indicators/definitions [Accessed 4 September 2018].

HESA, 2018b. *Who's studying in HE: Student enrolment by personal characteristics 2012/13–2016/17* [online]. Available from: www.hesa.ac.uk/data-and-analysis/students/whos-in-he [Accessed 4 September 2018].

HESA, 2018c. *Who's studying in HE: HE student enrolments by personal characteristics 2012/13 to 2016/17* [online]. Available from: www.hesa.ac.uk/data-and-analysis/students/whos-in-he [Accessed 4 September 2018].

Lingwood, R., 2015. Recovering from ELQ: A Cambridge view. *In*: Hillman, N., ed. *It's the finance, stupid! The decline of part-time higher education and what to do about it.* London: HEPI, 77–84.

Mee, K. and Wright, S., 2009. Geographies of belonging. *Environment and Planning A*, 41, 772–779.

Oxford Economics, 2014. *Macroeconomic influences on the demand for part-time higher education in the UK: Report to HEFCE* [online]. Available from: www.hefce.ac.uk/media/hefce/content/pubs/indirreports/2014/Macroeconomic,influences,on,the,demand,for,PT,HE/2014_ptdemand.pdf [Accessed 6 October 2015].

Rose-Adams, J., 2012. *Leaving university early: a research report from the back on course project.* Milton Keynes: The Open University.

Thomas, K., 2015. Rethinking belonging through Bourdieu, diaspora and the spatial. *Widening Participation and Lifelong Learning*, 17 (1), 37–48.

Trow, M., 1989. The Robbins trap: British attitudes and the limits of expansion. *Higher education quarterly*, 43 (1), 55–75

Universities UK, 2013. *The power of part-time: Review of part-time and mature higher education.* London: Universities UK.

3 A journey into border territory

Introduction

In previous chapters I have outlined the way in which the powerful narrative of belonging within UK retention literature assumes a young, full-time, time-rich undergraduate, resident on or close to campus. I argued that this narrative is problematic in two ways: first, that it promotes a reductive and exclusive understanding of belonging in the context of a diverse contemporary student body, including mature part-time undergraduates, a heterogeneous cohort who have become increasingly peripherally positioned in the English HE sector, and, second, that it articulates a direct association between belonging in HE and student retention, juxtaposing a linear, institution-centric measurement with a phenomenon far less tangible and within a highly stratified and complex space. In pursuit of 'thorough theorising of belonging . . . the differences between a sense of belonging, practices of belonging and formal structures of belonging' (Mee and Wright 2009, p. 774), this chapter now introduces the strategy of borderland analysis, the principle of which is to link multiple theories 'to portray a more complete picture of student identity' (Abes 2012, p. 190).

The characteristics of a borderland analysis

As researchers, too often we search for a final reckoning, which reduces complexity to an abstraction, but in a borderland analysis, tensions which arise from encounters on such theoretical borderlands are as welcome as synergies; they energise the researcher into 'letting go of monolithic beliefs . . . and acknowledging contradictory perspectives that speak to the multiplicity of students' experiences' (Abes 2009, p. 150). Abes's work is located within US student development theory which has evolved from a concern to measure the impact of student participation in the institution (Tinto 1975, 1987, 1989; Astin 1975, Pace 1984 *inter alia*) to accommodate the rapidly shifting cultural terrain on US college and university campuses, where social locations of race, gender and sexual orientation are of growing salience in the student experience.

(Tanaka 2002, p. 266)

This field of research is not precisely replicated in the UK, but its broad themes are represented in institutional preoccupations with student engagement, retention, success and belonging and a rich body of literature on multiple aspects of widening participation in HE (Burke, Hayton and Stevenson 2018; Moore, Sanders and Higham 2013; Kettley 2007 *inter alia*).

Abes's strategy of borderland analysis reflects Tanaka's critique that prevailing models of student development theory

had (1) an interest in measuring the impact of student participation in the institution and (2) a tendency *not* to examine the underlying cultures of that institution (often Western European, straight, upper middle class and male).

(Tanaka 2002, p. 264 original italics)

Abes is influenced by post-modernist approaches notably Lather's argument for 'a freeing rather than a containment of difference . . . a multiplicity of paradigms is necessary given the multiplicity of reality' (2007, p. 47) and the principles of bricolage, that is

methodological practices explicitly based on notions of eclecticism, emergent design, flexibility and plurality . . . approaches that examine phenomena from multiple, and sometimes competing, theoretical and methodological perspectives.

(Rogers 2012, p. 1)

What makes Abes's work distinctive, however, is her intention to work in theoretical borderlands *between* multiple paradigms, influenced by Gloria Anzaldúa's argument for a non-dualistic, 'both/and' identity. A scholar of Chicana cultural theory, feminist theory and queer theory, the prose and poetry of Anzaldúa's semi-autobiographical work *Borderlands/La Frontera: The New Mestiza* (1987) draws on her experiences of growing up as a lesbian woman of colour on the Texas/Mexico border. She argues against fixed positions of binary thought and states of being, simultaneously distilling the experiences of individuals occupying a rich territory of 'space between' and problematising the power relationships defining that space. In doing so, Anzaldúa gives shape to a third space, a new location 'where individuals fluctuate between two discrete worlds, participating in both and wholly belonging to neither' (Abes 2009, p. 528).

Concerned that conventional and singular analyses failed to address under-lying power structures impacting lesbian student identity on a US university campus, Abes partners two potentially contradictory perspectives, construc-tivism and queer theory, in order to 'focus increased attention on inequi-table power structures that result in oppressions such as racism, classism, and heterosexism' (*ibid.*, p. 143). She admits that 'these two theories were an unlikely and potentially problematic couple . . . because unlike constructiv-ism which focuses on how students experience their identities, queer theory challenges the notion of identity itself' (*ibid.*, p. 146). However, the aim is not to synthesise different theoretical positions and concepts but, rather, to value both synergies and productive tensions in the interdisciplinary spaces between distinct approaches. This requires the researcher to 'straddle mul-tiple theories using ideas from each to portray a more complete picture of identity . . . a new theoretical space' (Abes 2012, p. 190). A borderland analy-sis thrives on complexity and multiplicity. It 'challenges educators to . . . genuinely live and work within a context of multiple realities rather than trying to understand identity through tidy frameworks' (Abes 2009, p. 150).

> Both constructivism and queer theory provide a rich, yet incomplete perspective . . . together, they tell a richer story than either alone. . . . The queer/constructivist borderland brings to life students' lived expe-riences through constructivism while simultaneously deconstructing them through queer theory . . . we needed to simultaneously embrace both theoretical perspectives, despite their contradictory nature . . . to explain how we understood . . . development as simultaneously linear and nonlinear.
>
> (*ibid.*, p. 148)

Borderlands and belonging?

I adopt Abes's principle of partnering different and potentially contradictory perspectives in a borderland analysis of student belonging in HE, but I adapt her practice by bringing together the work of three individual theorists. This borderland analysis challenges the tempting dazzle of the binary: traditional/non-traditional, belonging/not-belonging. It allows for an interrogation of inequitable power structures within the UK HE sector and for exploration of ways in which these impact on student experiences. It makes room for complexity: the diversity of the student cohort and how particular groups, including mature part-time undergraduates, are positioned differently in the sector and thus experience the spaces of the university. A borderland analysis has the potential to move us towards an understanding of belonging as relational, contested, negotiated and in process.

Abes partners different theoretical perspectives: constructivism and queer theory. This borderland analysis generates a dialogue among Pierre Bourdieu, philosopher and sociologist; Avtar Brah, pioneer of Diaspora Studies; and Doreen Massey, radical geographer. My intention is to establish a new theoretical and methodological space in the borderlands between different ways of seeing – geographical and sociological, psychosocial and post-colonial – to break out of 'the typical paradigmatic categories into which studies are generally categorized' (Abes 2009, p. 142). Each theorist brings spatiality to the table. Each demonstrates interdisciplinarity in considering relations of power in space. Individually complex and rich, Bourdieu's, Brah's and Massey's ideas become richer in dialogue, enabling an interrogation of student belonging in HE through ideas of space and power.

References

Abes, L., 2009. Theoretical borderlands: Using multiple theoretical perspectives to challenge inequitable power structures in student development theory. *Journal of College Student Development*, 50 (2), 141–156.

Abes, L., 2012. Constructivist and intersectional interpretations of a lesbian college student's multiple social identities. *Journal of Higher Education*, 83 (2), 186–216.

Anzaldúa, G., 1987. *Borderlands/La Frontera: The New Mestiza*. San Francisco: Aunt Lute Books.

Astin, A.W., 1975. *Preventing students from dropping out*. San Francisco: Jossey-Bass.

Burke, P.J., Hayton, A. and Stevenson, J., 2018. *Evaluating equity and widening participation in higher education*. Stoke-on-Trent: Trentham Books.

Kettley, N., 2007. The past, present and future of widening participation research. *British Journal of Sociology of Education*, 28 (3), 333–347.

Lather, P., 2007. *Getting lost: Feminist efforts towards a double(d) science*. New York: State University of New York Press.

Mee, K. and Wright, S., 2009. Geographies of belonging. *Environment and planning A*, 41, 772–779.

Moore, J., Sanders, J. and Higham, L., 2013. *Literature review of research into widening participation to higher education*. Report to HEFCE by ARC Network August 2013. Bristol: HEFCE.

Pace, C.R., 1984. *Measuring the quality of college student experience*. Los Angeles: UCLA Higher Education Research Institute.

Rogers, M., 2012. Contextualizing theories and practices of bricolage research. *The Qualitative Report*, 17, 1–17 [online]. Available from: www.nova.edu/ssss/QR/QR17/rogers.pdf [Accessed 15 May 2015].

Tanaka, G., 2002. Higher education's self-reflexive turn: Towards an intercultural theory of student development. *The Journal of Higher Education*, 73 (2), 263–296.

Tinto, V., 1975. Dropout from higher education: A theoretical synthesis of recent research. *Review of Educational Research*, 45, 89–125.

Tinto, V., 1987. *Leaving college: Rethinking the causes and cures of student attrition.* Chicago, IL: University of Chicago Press.

Tinto, V., 1989. Stages of student departure: Reflections on the longitudinal character of student leaving. *Journal of Higher Education*, 59, 438–455.

4 Borderlands and belonging

Introduction

This chapter is the theoretical heart of this book. It establishes a rich theoretical space for rethinking student belonging in HE. This borderland analysis presents, in dialogue, a Bourdieusian analysis of belonging as relational, Brah's concepts of diaspora and diaspora space which emphasise the psychosocial dimension of belonging and Massey's spatial concepts and tools framing space and power as fluid and contested. These theorise belonging 'in a way which articulates differential power relationships at work within the HE sector and in universities' (Thomas 2015)

It is the nature of academic publication to tidily present what was, in practice, an incremental, sometimes messy, thinking process. For the reader's sake, this chapter reflects a broadly chronological overview of the construction of this borderland analysis, beginning with an outline of Bourdieusian individual habitus in or out of alignment with the structured social space of the academy. It then addresses the psychosocial dimension of belonging and a nuanced articulation of lived experience encapsulated in Brah's concepts of diaspora and diaspora space (1996). Third, the chapter examines Massey's spatial concepts, emphasising plurality, temporality and flux. The chapter concludes by establishing the structuring themes of the borderlands between Bourdieu, Brah and Massey: space and power.

Bourdieu: belonging as relational

In multiple analyses of twentieth-century French society (Bourdieu 1988a, 1988b, 2005; Bourdieu and Passeron 1977 *inter alia*) Bourdieu argues that education reproduces material advantage and disadvantage, which 'fulfils its social function of conservation and its ideological function of legitimation' (Bourdieu and Passeron 1977, p. 102). He claims his theoretical framework has the capacity 'to uncover the most deeply buried structures of the different social worlds . . . as well as the "mechanisms" that tend to ensure their reproduction' (1996, p. 1). Habitus, capital and field are the perhaps the best known and most widely operationalised of Bourdieu's conceptual tools across a wide range of academic disciplines.

> For Bourdieusian scholars, his conceptual tools (habitus, capital, field, practice) provide a language to articulate experiences and a theoretical orientation in research . . . Bourdieusian scholars . . . have a level of deep, enduring respect for his efforts to devise a conceptual toolbox, to bridge the theory/method divide.
>
> (Stahl 2016, p. 1094)

Bourdieusian analyses have been widely modelled in research which aims to 'understand and theorise changing policies and practices in education, including tertiary and higher education' (Bathmaker 2015, p. 65).

Bourdieu uses the spatial metaphor the 'field' to 'uncover the workings of power and inequality in particular social spaces' (Bathmaker 2015, p. 65). Social agents – individuals, groups or institutions – employ strategies to hold or enhance their position in 'the field of power . . . structurally determined by the state of the relations of power among . . . different forms of capital' (Bourdieu 1998, p. 264). Fields of power – the state, industry, culture, education – contain multiple subfields, of which HE is one. A field analysis 'allows for an exploration of space, whether social or physical as relational' (Stahl 2016, p. 1097). Bourdieu reinforces the contested nature and spatial dimensions of 'field' through three distinctive metaphors: a field of play, a force field and a self-contained world.

Position in the field is determined by cultural capital (Bourdieu and Passeron 1977), a concept fundamental to Bourdieu's project of demonstrating how social inequality is reproduced in both economic and symbolic spheres. Distinct from economic capital or wealth, cultural capital exists in three forms: embodied (within the person as predispositions and lifestyle choices), objectified (in artefacts and books) and institutionalised (formal education). Individuals acquire more or less cultural capital over time, enabling them to navigate a field by knowing the 'rules of the game'. 'Positions in the field then produce in agents and institutions particular ways of thinking, being and doing' (Bathmaker 2015, p. 66), developing what is termed 'habitus'.

Bourdieu defines habitus as 'the social inscribed in the body of the biological individual' (Bourdieu 1985, p. 113), meaning the systems of dispositions of individuals, groups and institutions, structured by past and present circumstances and which structure present and future practices. Habitus is internalised and cemented during early life within family and educational structures:

> The habitus acquired within the family forms the basis of the reception and assimilation of the classroom message, and the habitus acquired at school conditions the level of reception and degree of assimilation of the messages produced and diffused by the culture industry.
>
> (*ibid.*, p. 43)

Habitus implies that individuals instinctively understand and feel 'at home' in the environment in which they are born and brought up; they experience an 'unproblematic alignment between the dispositions of the habitus and the demands of the field' (Reay, Crozier and Clayton 2009, p. 1112). 'When habitus encounters a social world of which it is the product, it is like a "fish in water": it does not feel the weight of the water and it takes the world about itself for granted' (Bourdieu and Wacquant 1992, p. 127). The metaphor not only is a powerful expression of the perceived effortless of belonging but also implies the deeply uncomfortable experience of not belonging. Habitus is in relation with the field so that 'practices are not simply the result of one's habitus but rather of relations between one's habitus and one's current circumstances' (Maton 2008, p. 52). Habitus 'sets a potentially infinite number of patterns of behaviour, thought and expression that are both relatively unpredictable but also limited in their diversity' (Bourdieu 1990, p. 5). One manifestation of this limitation is self-exclusion: 'a sense of one's place which leads one to exclude oneself from places where one is excluded' (1988a, p. 471).

Considering HE as a field of play imagines it as 'a boundaried site where a . . . competitive game is played' (Thomson 2008, p. 68), but the playing field is not level; 'players who begin with particular forms of capital are advantaged at the outset because the field depends on or produces more of that capital' (*ibid.*, p. 69). Applying the metaphor of a force field to HE, reflects inherent internal conflicts between economic and symbolic capitals; not only is the field uneven, advantaging those who enter with greater capital, but the UK sector also reflects 'a hierarchy of privilege, with unequal funding and . . . a stigma of blame attached to institutions lower in a pecking order determined by historical criteria, leading to tensions and fragmentations' (McNay 2006, p. 9). Finally, although HE is a semi-autonomous subfield of the wider field of education, as 'a separate universe governed by its own laws' (Bourdieu 2005, p. 5) it maintains inherent conventions, principles and hierarchies of disciplinary and academic tradition and determines terms of entry that are key to its reproduction. Unlike the elite, the tightly homogenous field of the twentieth-century French academy in which Bourdieu spent much of his professional life, contemporary UK HE has experienced 'increasing heteronomy, increasing control of the field from forces outside the field . . . associated with expansion and diversification' (Bathmaker 2015, p. 67). Heteronomy itself leads to power struggles within the field.

A Bourdieusian theorising of belonging is rooted in social structures and worlds, with habitus, capital and field as 'an inter-dependent and co-constructed trio' (Thomson 2008, p. 69) at its heart. The habitus of young middle-class people predisposes them to experience a sense of belonging in a traditional or elite HE environment: 'as if it was "natural", where they hold a cultural and educational "entitlement", true "citizens" of the UK HE system' (Stuart, Lido and Morgan 2011, p. 506). Those whose habitus is not aligned with traditional practices of HE – mature, working-class and minority ethnic students, for example – are perceived and perceive themselves as 'other' in an elite HE environment. Where there is a mismatch between habitus and field, 'individuals experience 'a sense of uncertainty and feelings of anxiety' (Reay, Crozier and Clayton 2010, p. 117). Research on nine working-class students at an 'elite' university found that the students' schooling 'did not provide easy access to forms of dominant cultural capital sanctioned and recognized by the educational system' (*ibid.*, p. 1105), and, on arrival at the university, the students experienced 'the shock of the elite' (*ibid.*, p. 1111). *Paired Peers* (2013; Bathmaker *et al.* 2016), a longitudinal study of working-class and middle-class undergraduates at two universities, employs Bourdieusian conceptual tools to investigate 'how students' class backgrounds impacted on their choices, experiences and achievements' (University of Bristol 2018) and to better understand the way students mobilise and generate different forms of capital to enhance their future social position.

Read, Archer and Leathwood (2003) argue that mature, working-class and minority ethnic students often choose to apply to post-1992 universities in order to increase their chances of belonging in academic culture. They perceive these institutions as those in which students from a range of ethnic backgrounds, ages or classes can feel they belong without being reduced to special cases, often through the presence of significant numbers of students 'like me' (*ibid.*, p. 266). Thus, students act

> within the field, as more or less 'knowing agents', viewing HE as: a privilege, a right or a necessity, depending on a variety of structural factors such as social class, race, gender and disability, which position them differently in relation to expectations about participation in HE.
>
> (Bathmaker and Thomas 2009, p. 119)

Yet even in a system of mass HE, academic culture sustains a dominant discourse of the authentic student as White and middle-class and the first-year entrant 'as a school-leaver with little or no familial responsibilities' (Read *et al.* 2003, pp. 261–265). This discourse has survived several decades of widening participation policy and continues to be reflected in the narrative of retention and belonging.

A Bourdieusian analysis conceptualises of student belonging in HE as a practice and a product of the relations of power embedded in a stratified sector, constructed around the privileged identities of the 'typical' or 'authentic' student: young and full-time. The strengths of this analysis are in emphasising 'the relational: individual and group interactions with social structure, not individual deficit' (Thomas 2015, p. 41).

> What Bourdieu does write about . . . is being exposed to the world. . . that we develop dispositions in response to that exposure . . . the confrontation between the habitus and the field is always marked by affectivity, by affective transactions between habitus and the field . . . the mutual constitution of the individual and the social relations within which they are enmeshed . . . deepen and enrich notions of habitus.
>
> (Reay 2015, pp. 10–12)

Meanwhile, a 'new generation' of scholars use

> Bourdieusian theory in interrogating social realities in a contemporary context . . . putting Bourdieu to work . . . celebrate the use of Bourdieu's thinking tools in ways in which he, himself, did not, including migration, 'race'/ethnicity and gender.
>
> (Burke, Thatcher, Ingram and Abrahams 2015, p. 1)

For example, Wallace examines 'Black' cultural capital, claiming 'Bourdieu's penetrating scrutiny of contemporary class arrangements afforded me the relevant language to think about racialized taste and style distinctions across and within class' (2015, p. 38).

He notes 'there are communities of scholars for whom the extension of cultural capital to consider "race" and ethnicity more significantly may be an unbearable stretch of Bourdieu's theory of social practice' (*ibid.*, p. 52). Like the new generation of scholars, I could have chosen to 'stretch' a Bourdieusian analysis to better reflect what I felt was still unaccounted for: the heterogeneity of the contemporary student population, the possibility of alternative negotiated versions of feeling 'at home' and 'the pleasures and pain associated with gender, class and sexuality – the affective aspects of inequality' (Skeggs 1997, p. 9). I chose instead to rethink belonging by building on the basis of individuals' relationships with their environment but to search for a more convincing articulation of the psychosocial in that interaction. Brah's articulation of this dimension (1996) forms the second element of this borderland analysis.

Brah: the diasporic dynamic

Brah's concept of diaspora builds a bridge between Bourdieu's schematic social framework and complex lived experience in contested space. Brah is a sociologist of race, ethnicity, gender and identity, a pioneer in the field of Diaspora Studies (Brah and Clini 2017, p. 163). Her ideas are shaped by feminist and post-colonial theory and informed by personal experiences of displacement and migration:

> I was born in Panjab and went to Uganda at the age of about six. Uganda was still a colony or a 'protectorate' to be precise. I became aware of the social and psychological impact of the simultaneous positionality of dominance and subordination, and of the complex entanglements of colonial power hierarchies. I became a refugee when Idi Amin expelled Asians from Uganda and I could not return. . . . My identity of 'Ugandan of Asian origin' provided me with a means of reflection on the nature of hybrid identities and the power dynamics that underpin them.
>
> (*ibid.*, pp. 163–164)

In historical contexts of diaspora 'hitherto sharply differentiated cultures and people . . . are forced to interact, often in profoundly asymmetrical ways in terms of their relative power' (Massey and Jess 1995, p. 193). While commonly associated with contexts of race and post-colonial theory the use of the term 'diaspora' is expanding 'a growing body of literature succeeded in reformulating the definition, framing diaspora as almost any *population* on the move and no longer referring to the specific *context* of their existence' (Weinar 2010, p. 75, original italics). My own translation of diaspora to the question of belonging in HE is also a translation and reformulation inspired by the richness of diaspora as 'a heuristic device to think about questions of home, belonging, continuity and community' (Fortier 2001, p. 406) in the context of a diverse student population.

Brah conceptualises 'diaspora' as 'an interpretive frame for analysing the economic political and cultural modalities of historically specific forms of migrancy' (1996, p. 15) but in a way that frees the concept from 'particular maps and histories' (Clifford 1994, p. 303). Brah is interested not only 'in who travels, but when, how and under what circumstances' (1996, p. 189).

She maps contested territories and trajectories of privilege and disadvantage in social contexts. The engine of the diasporic dynamic is power. In a process of relational positioning, 'regimes of power differentiate one group from another to represent them as similar or different; to include or exclude them from constructions of the "nation" and the body politic' (*ibid.*, p. 180). Diasporic journeys are not casual or temporary; they are 'essentially about settling down, about putting roots elsewhere . . . are potentially the sites of hope and new beginnings' (*ibid.*, p. 190). Whether transformation is realised can depend on the way the in which the traveller is situated by the regime(s) of power at his or her destination: 'how and in what ways is a group inserted within the social relations of class, gender, racism, sexuality or other axes of differentiation in the country to which it migrates?' (*ibid.*, p. 179).

Viewed through a diasporic lens, regimes of power within HE are driven by pressing market and institution-centric agendas: student retention, student satisfaction and league table ranking, relationally position those who risk those agendas as problem or target groups. Part-time undergraduates are one such group, a population declining in numbers, occupying strategically precarious space in HE territory and performing less than well in sector metrics. They are 'marked by the multiplicity of subject positions that constitute a subject' (*ibid.*, p. 123), negotiating a learner identity alongside multiple and prioritised identities (Jackson 2008) as employee, parent, carer, citizen. Their student identity differs from their younger, full-time peers; they are 'students who live at home, are part-time, older and/or are on courses with extended contact/workplace hours' (Thomas 2012, p. 6), hybrid modes of engagement which, it *What Works?* argues, inhibit participation, integration and belonging in HE.

Brah's concept of diaspora problematises the possibility of developing a sense of belonging in spaces shaped by differentiated power relations. Relational positioning shapes 'the lived experience of a locality . . . the same geographical space comes to articulate different histories and meanings, such that "home" can simultaneously be a place of safety and terror' (Brah 1996, p. 204). The psychosocial dimension of 'diaspora' describes the lived experience of locality, not only the uneven distribution of power in contested spaces but also the complexity of lived experience in those spaces: a succession of stories of (re)settlement, encounters, emotional ties, work, love, sweat and tears (Fortier 2001, p. 145). To identify what is shared with some inevitably involves the identification of 'the other'. Identification with a group 'is constructed on the back of a recognition of some common origin or shared characteristics . . . or with an ideal and with the natural closure of solidarity and allegiance established on this foundation' (Hall 2000, p. 17). The nature of belonging is therefore exclusive as well as inclusive.

Brah also proposes a companion concept: diaspora space:

> the intersectionality of diaspora, border and dis/location inhabited not only by those who have migrated . . . but equally by those who are constructed and represented as indigenous . . . and who occupy the indigene subject position as the privileged space of legitimate claims of belonging.
>
> (Brah 1996, p. 178)

Let us imagine HE as a diaspora space, with the 'typical' undergraduate, full-time and young, as the 'indigenous' occupant, and non-traditional students, including part-time (and) mature undergraduates, as diasporic populations with contested claims to belonging. All new undergraduates are initially displaced and must orientate themselves within a new environment, investing university spaces with meaning through interaction with them. Cashmore, Scott and Cane (2011) found that undergraduates reported a high degree of sense of belonging to a particular place within the university, most usually a departmental building or a small campus. Investing meaning in space which transforms it into 'place' requires commitment and anticipates a return; it is an affective process closely associated with belonging, 'the desire for more than what is . . . for some sort of attachment' (Probyn 1996, p. 6).

'Yet HE and its campuses are not neutral spaces. They are ruled and boundaried by the power relationships of the academy and the sector' (Thomas 2015, p. 43). The concept of diaspora space allows opportunities for transformation and reconstitution 'via a multitude of border crossings . . . territorial, political, economic, cultural and psychological' (*ibid.*, p. 206). So for some, the spaces of the university or the campus in which they invest to gain a sense of attachment may peripheral to glossy social learning spaces, sports fields or student bars. Brah argues that those interactions have the capacity and potential to 'thoroughly re-inscribe space . . . it is continually reconstituted' (*ibid.*) with the potential for new negotiated forms of identity and alternative practices of belonging.

Bourdieu and Brah: the borderlands?

There are clear differences and tensions between the ideas and identities of Bourdieu and Brah. Bourdieu, a twentieth-century Parisian academic and public intellectual with experience of French military service in the Algerian war of independence (Grenfell 2008, p. 13), understates gender and race:

> works such as *The Algerians* (1962) and *Weight of the World* (2003) shed some light on Bourdieu's sensitivity to ethnicity, migration and

displacement as social factors that complicate class hierarchies. Yet even within the above mentioned works, Bourdieu's class conscious-ness is 'race light' at best.

(Wallace 2015, p. 38)

Brah is a feminist woman of colour whose life trajectory has taken her across several continents as a migrant, refugee and academic (Brah and Clini 2017). Her work is grounded in conditions of post-colonial migration in a mobile, globalised world. What they share, however, is an interest in articu-lating the mutual interaction of individuals with their social environment in which power is unequally distributed. In the context of student belonging in HE, a Bourdieusian field analysis sets a template for individuals' interac-tions in the structured social space of HE; Brah's diasporic dynamic maps the nuanced psychosocial dimensions of the academy, the campus and the classroom, 'conveying the complexity of lived experience and inequality' (Thomas 2015). In dialogue, their perspectives offer a more agile analysis of the power dynamics within a volatile sector and diverse population than Bourdieu's arguably over-schematic framework which 'risks homogenising internally diverse social groups' (*ibid.*, p. 42). Together, they reinforce a sense of belonging as inherently geographical, shaped by space and power. In considering how to theoretically (re)imagine such spaces I turned to the work of Doreen Massey, and this became the third element of this border-land analysis of belonging in HE.

Massey: thinking spatially

Massey, a radical geographer, writing on space, place and power (1991, 1993, 1994, 2005*inter alia*) brings Marxist and feminist perspectives to geo-graphical scholarship. She engages with feminist and gender debates from the perspective of spatiality as the product of intersecting social relations (1994), sustaining a feminist geographic agenda to explore ways in which

specific spaces . . . are produced and stabilised by the dominant groups who occupy them, such that they develop hegemonic cultures through which power operates to systematically define ways of being and to mark out those who are in place or out of place.

(Valentine 2008, p. 18)

Massey is a key figure in the diverse project of feminist geography which aims 'to investigate, make visible and challenge the relationships between gender divisions and spatial divisions, to uncover their mutual constitution to problematise their apparent naturalness' (McDowell 1999, p. 12).

Her approach to space is based on three propositions: that space is the product of interrelations on multiple scales, that distinct and heterogeneous trajectories coexist in space and that space is always under construction. She argues for space as inherently temporal and against the philosophical separation of these dimensions, claiming that this reinforces 'the imagination of the spatial as petrification . . . a safe haven from the temporal . . . the notion of space as surface. All these imaginaries diminish our understanding of spatiality' (2005, p. 28). She emphasises the temporality of space in the term *space-time* and applies the characteristics of space to her definition of place, not as a fixed entity but as something much more fluid: 'a particular articulation of those relations, a particular moment in those networks of social relations and understandings' (1994, p. 5). 'If space is as a simultaneity of stories-so-far then places are collections of those stories' (2005, p. 130). Understanding space as the site of coexisting, heterogeneous trajectories disrupts ideas of place as stable, as somewhere to return to, and of culture and identity as bounded and closed. For example, Massey describes the neighbourhood of Kilburn, London: 'it is absolutely not a seamless, coherent identity, a single sense of place which everyone shares. . . . People's routes through the place, their favourite haunts within it, the connections the make (physically, or by phone or post, or in memory and imagination) between here and the rest of the world . . . vary enormously' (1994, p. 153).

Whereas power is central to Bourdieu's and Brah's theorising of social contexts, Massey claims space itself is the product of social relations shaped by power. She argues that places are 'extroverted', in that 'a large proportion of . . . relations, experiences and understandings are constructed on a far larger scale than what we happen to define for that moment as the place itself' (2005, p. 141). She applies this in multiple contexts, including the academy, part of a 'network of specialised places of knowledge production (elite; historically largely male) which gained (and continues to gain) at least a part of its prestige from the cachet and exclusivity of its spatiality' (*ibid.*, p. 75). Individual universities are themselves points of articulation of multiple social relations, each a node in the wider geography of the academy pulling on identities and connections beyond their geographical boundaries. HE is a space of social relations shaped by patriarchy, tradition, academic and disciplinary discourses, economics and government, a power geometry in which

> different social groups, and different individuals, are placed in very distinct ways in relation to these flows and interconnections . . . some people are more in charge of it than others; some initiate flows and movement, others don't.
>
> (Massey 1991)

Massey theorises the academy as 'an emerging, violently unequal, twenty-first-century geography of, a particular form of, knowledge' (2005, p. 143), with individual universities as points of articulation of social relations, nodes in that geography, each an extroverted place, constructed through the wider social relations of the sector. There are synergies here with a Bourdieusian field analysis of HE: as a structured social space characterised by internal conflict and an uneven distribution of advantage based on the accumulation and reproduction of capital. If place is unfixed, in process our relationships with place are in flux too. A native of Cumbria and a keen hiker in her spare time, Massey writes, 'The rocks of Skiddaw are immigrant rocks, just passing through here and changing all the while . . . we can't, on a weekend in the country, go back to nature. It too is moving on' (*ibid.*, p. 137). This problematises the idea of belonging as universal, bounded to and within an institutional space. It also questions 'conceiving space as a static slice through time, as representation, as a closed system . . . are all ways of taming it' (*ibid.*, p. 59) which problematises linear, time-bound definitions of retention. Massey argues instead for a progressive sense of place (1994), one open to negotiation and change:

> Is it not possible for a sense of place to be progressive; not self-closing and defensive, but outward-looking? A sense of place, an understanding of 'its character', which can only be constructed by linking that place to places beyond? A progressive sense of place would recognize that, without being threatened by it.
>
> (Massey 1994)

There is clear synergy between Massey's progressive sense of place and Brah's diaspora space, both imagining a far wider and more flexible territory in which connection, attachment, belonging may be negotiated and generated. This transformative potential characterises the borderlands between the two and is crucial in moving this borderland analysis beyond a critique and towards a re-imagination of the prevailing narrative of belonging.

Including Massey in this borderland analysis of student belonging also introduces the heuristic device of activity space, 'the spatial network of links and activities, of spatial connections and of locations, within which a particular agent operates . . . within each activity space there is a geography of power' (Massey 2005, p. 55). This device challenges the idea of place as stable and coherent, capturing power dynamics and complexity without and within. It raises questions about how institutional spaces inhabited and by whom. What geographies of power construct differential claims to belonging? Understanding 'the university' as an activity space complements both a Bourdieusian analysis of HE as a relational, stratified field and a diasporic dynamic of relational positioning in which particular groups are identified as 'different' or 'other'. The way in which activity space was put to work in this study is outlined in more detail in the next chapter.

Space and power: a borderland analysis of student belonging

Abes's intention in developing a borderland analysis is to link multiple theories in order 'to portray a more complete picture of student identity' (Abes 2012, p. 190). This borderland places the ideas of Bourdieu, Brah and Massey in dialogue, to generate a multilayered analysis of a complex phenomenon – student belonging – compatible with the contemporary diversity of the student body. It establishes a wider and more complex territory for belonging in theoretical borderlands between Bourdieu, Brah and Massey. The principal themes of the dialogue, and therefore of this borderland analysis are space and power. Synergies between a Bourdieusian field analysis, Brah's dynamic of relational positioning and Massey's geographies of power foreground the lived experiences of relationships of power in space, 'using ideas from each to portray a more complete picture of identity . . . a new theoretical space' (Abes 2012, p. 190). Differences of emphasis, as well as unanticipated synergies, expose an understanding of student belonging in HE to greater analytical complexity.

This borderland analysis critiques the prevailing, taken-for-granted narrative through problematising the naturalness of spatial relations in HE. It positions the sector and 'the university' as sites of power and knowledge in which narratives are articulated and identities constructed, resulting in different lived experiences within those sites. Significantly, however, Brah's concept of diaspora space and Massey's argument for a progressive sense of place take this borderland analysis beyond critique, beyond a binary of belonging/not-belonging. There is potential 'for transformation and progress in conceiving of space as "a simultaneity of stories-so-far"' (Thomas 2015) in which diasporic themes of journey, displacement and home interact with physical, political and emotional space. The structuring device of activity space opens theoretical and methodological space for re-imagining student belonging in HE.

References

Abes, L., 2012. Constructivist and intersectional interpretations of a lesbian college student's multiple social identities. *Journal of Higher Education*, 83 (2), 186–216.
Bathmaker, A.-M., 2015. Thinking with Thinking after Bourdieu: Using 'field' to consider in/equalities in the changing field of English higher education. *Cambridge Journal of Education*, 45 (1), 61–80.

Bathmaker, A.-M., Ingram, N., Abrahams, J., Hoare, A., Waller, R. and Bradley, H., 2016. *Higher education, social class and social mobility: The degree generation.* London: Palgrave MacMillan.

Bathmaker, A.-M. and Thomas, W., 2009. Positioning themselves: An exploration of the nature and meaning of transitions in the context of dual sector FE/HE institutions in England. *Journal of Further and Higher Education,* 33 (2), 119–130.

Bourdieu, P., 1985. From rules to strategies: An interview with Pierre Bourdieu. *Cultural Anthropology,* 1, 110–120.

Bourdieu, P., 1988a. *State nobility: Elite schools in the field of power.* Cambridge: Polity Press.

Bourdieu, P., 1988b. *Homo academicus,* translated by P. Collier. Cambridge: Polity Press (1984).

Bourdieu, P., 1990. *The logic of practice,* translated by R. Nice. Cambridge: Polity Press (1980).

Bourdieu, P., 1996. *The rules of art: Genesis and structure of the literary field.* Redwood City, CA: Stanford University Press.

Bourdieu, P., 1998. *On television and journalism.* London: Pluto (1996).

Bourdieu, P., 2005. *The social structures of the economy.* Cambridge: Polity Press.

Bourdieu, P. and Passeron, J.C., 1977. *Reproduction in education, society and culture.* London: Sage.

Bourdieu, P. and Wacquant, L., 1992. *An invitation to reflexive sociology,* translated by L. Wacquant. Cambridge: Polity Press.

Brah, A., 1996. *Cartographies of disapora: Contesting identities.* London: Routledge.

Brah, A. and Clini, C., 2017. Contemporary feminist discourses and practices within and across boundaries: an interview with Avtar Brah. *Feminist Review,* 100 (1), 163–170.

Burke, C., Thatcher, J., Ingram, N. and Abrahams, J., 2015. The development of Bourdieu's intellectual heritage in UK sociology. *In:* Thatcher, J., Ingram, N., Burke, C. and Abrahams, J., eds. *Bourdieu: The next generation.* London: Routledge, 1–7.

Cashmore, A., Scott, J. and Cane, C., 2011. 'Belonging' and 'intimacy' factors in the retention of students: An investigation into the student perceptions of effective practice and how that practice can be replicated. *In: What works? Student retention and success.* York: HEA.

Clifford, J., 1994. Diasporas. *Cultural Anthropology,* 9 (3), 302–338.

Fortier, A.-M., 2001. 'Coming home': Queer migrations and multiple evocations of home. *European Journal of Cultural Studies,* 4 (4), 405–424.

Grenfell, M., ed., 2008. *Pierre Bourdieu: Key concepts.* Stocksfield: Acumen.

Hall, S., 2000. Who needs 'identity'? *In:* du Gay, P., Evans, J. and Redman, P., eds. *Identity: A reader.* London: Sage.

Jackson, S., 2008. Diversity, identity and belonging: Women's spaces of sociality. *The International Journal of Diversity in Organisations, Communities and Nations,* 8 (3), 147–154.

Massey, D., 1991. A global sense of place. *Marxism Today*, June, 24–29.

Massey, D., 1993. Power geometry and a progressive sense of place. *In*: Bird, J., Curtis, B., Putnam, T. and Tickner, L., eds. *Mapping the futures: Local cultures, global change*. London: Routledge, 60–70.

Massey, D., 1994. *Space, place and gender*. Cambridge: Polity Press.

Massey, D., 2005. *For space*. London: Sage.

Massey, D. and Jess, P., 1995. *A place in the world? Places, cultures and globalisation*. Oxford: The Open University and Oxford University Press.

Maton, K., 2008. Habitus. *In*: Grenfell, M., ed. *Pierre Bourdieu: Key concepts*. Stocksfield: Acumen, 49–65.

McDowell, L., 1999. *Gender, identity and place: Understanding feminist geographies*. Cambridge: Polity Press.

McNay, I., ed., 2006. *Beyond mass higher education: Building on experience*. Maidenhead: SRHE and Open University Press.

Probyn, E., 1996. *Outside belongings*. New York and London: Routledge.

Read, B., Archer, L. and Leathwood, C., 2003. Challenging cultures? Student conceptions of 'belonging' and 'isolation' at a post-1992 university. *Studies in Higher Education*, 28 (3), 261–277.

Reay, D., 2015. Habitus and the psychosocial: Bourdieu with feelings. *Cambridge Journal of Education*, 45 (1), 9–23.

Reay, D., Crozier, G. and Clayton, J., 2009. Strangers in paradise? Working-class students in elite universities. *Sociology*, 43 (6), 1103–1121.

Reay, D., Crozier, G. and Clayton, J., 2010. 'Fitting in' or 'standing out': Working-class students in higher education. *British Educational Research Journal*, 36 (1), 107–124.

Skeggs, B., 1997. *Formations of class & gender*. London: Sage.

Stahl, G., 2016. Doing Bourdieu justice: Thinking with and beyond Bourdieu. *British Journal of Sociology of Education*, 37 (7), 1091–1103.

Stuart, M., Lido, C. and Morgan, J., 2011. Personal stories: How students' social and cultural life histories. *The Browne report, 2010: Securing a sustainable future for higher education: Independent review of higher education funding and student finance* [online]. London: Department of Business, Innovation & Skills.

Thomas, K., 2015. Rethinking belonging through Bourdieu, diaspora and the spatial. *Widening Participation and Lifelong Learning*, 17 (1), 37–48.

Thomas, L., 2012. *Engagement and belonging in higher education in a time of change: A summary of findings and recommendations from the what works? Student retention & success programme*. Executive Summary. Bristol: HEFCE.

Thomson, P., 2008. Field. *In*: Grenfell, M., ed. *Pierre Bourdieu: Key concepts*. Stocksfield: Acumen, 67–81.

University of Bristol, 2018. *Paired Peers* [online]. Available from: www.bristol.ac.uk/spais/research/paired-peers/report/ [Accessed 6 September 2018].

Valentine, G., 2008. Living with difference: Reflections on geographies of encounter. *Progress in Human Geography*, 32, 321–335.

Wallace, D.O., 2015. Re-interpreting Bourdieu, belonging and Black identities: Exploring 'Black' cultural capital among Black Caribbean youth in London. *In*: Thatcher, J., ed. *Bourdieu: The next generation*. London: Routledge.

Weinar, A., 2010. Instrumentalising diasporas for development: International and European policy discourses. *In*: Bauböck, R. and Faist, T., eds. *Diaspora and transnationalism: Concepts,theories and methods*. Amsterdam: Amsterdam University Press, 73–89.

5 Thinking spatially

Introduction

So far, I have written about rethinking student belonging through a borderland analysis as if it were a paper exercise. It was not. This book is the result of an empirical study, a multiple case study of four English universities involving 93 student participants and 25 staff participants (Thomas 2016). In this chapter, I outline the methodological strategy I developed to enact and reflect a borderland analysis of student belonging.

Thinking spatially

'Researching in the borderlands is worth the challenging methodological considerations that venturing into this new territory raises', writes Abes (2009, p. 155), for whom doing so led 'to rich new research results and possibilities' (*ibid.*, p. 141), 'personal changes and heightened awareness' (*ibid.*, p. 153). Having initiated a theoretical dialogue between themes of space, power and belonging, I required a congruent methodology, one sensitised to 'the social as inexorably also spatial' (Massey 1993, p. 80). How would my research methods capture the complexities of Bourdieu's socio-spatial relations, Brah's contested diaspora spaces and Massey's power geometry?

Methodologically as well as theoretically, a borderland analysis involves seeking new territory in productive tensions between multiple approaches. Massey urges us to 'think of spatiality in a highly active and politically enabling manner' (1993, p. 142), and thinking spatially proved central to this re-imagining of a complex phenomenon. Thinking spatially about student belonging invites attention to the spatial relationships of HE, considering how space is inhabited and by whom, uncovering power dynamics within the institution and in campus spaces. It provides a methodological language with which to articulate the ways in which institution and individual interact in uneven territory and highlights dominant and marginal practices of belonging. Thinking spatially is both abstract and applied. It influenced practices of data collection, analysis and authorship. It also informed my understanding of my role and identity as a researcher.

Case study as canvas

Case study offers a broad and flexible canvas on which to practise thinking spatially. As a method, it reflects the common characteristics of qualitative research: the significance of context and context-specific knowledge, the use of wide range of research methods in data collection and the positioning of the researcher as actively interpretive, seeking an understanding of subjective experience. Case study literature is crowded with typologies (Merriam 1991; Stake 1994; Yin 1994), but at its most generic, it is 'an empirical enquiry that . . . investigates a contemporary phenomenon within its real-life context' (Yin 1994, p. 13) through one or more cases 'within a bounded system' (Creswell 2007, p. 73), for example an organisation, an event or an individual. It is the range of evidence available to a case study which gives it its unique strength (Yin 1994). Case study relies on thick description, the interconnectedness of diverse aspects of social life, to show the full context of what is going on (Geertz 1993, p. 6), situating participants' experience and behaviour in the context in which these occur. The researcher acts as 'an interpreter in the field, to observe the workings of the case' (Stake 1995, p. 8).

This multiple case study corresponds to Stake's definition of 'instrumental', that is cases studied to provide insight into an issue; the case itself is of secondary interest. In a multiple case study of this type, 'understanding each case requires an understanding of other cases . . . but also an understanding of each one's uniqueness' (Stake 1994, p. 44). It therefore draws most closely on an idiographic approach, 'literally a writing of the particular local circumstances' (Crang 1998, p. 192) and described by Stake as 'the study of the particularity and complexity of a single case' . . . in which 'understanding the case is prioritised over generalising beyond it' (1995, p. xii). Given the diversity of the HE sector, part-time providers and part-time undergraduates, the selection of four case study universities aimed to identify 'exemplifying cases . . . not chosen because they are extreme or unusual in some way but because they will provide a suitable context for certain research questions to be answered' (Bryman 2004, p. 51). Each university in this study offers face-to-face, part-time provision and, at the time of selection, had 150 or more part-time entrants to first degrees in 2012. The four selected comprised three post-1992 universities – New Ecclesiastical, Northern City, Modern Eastern – and one pre-1992 university, Metropolitan Elite. The four varied in overall size and part-time population in order to achieve balance and variety (Stake 1995). I conducted a total of five group workshops and three individual interviews with mature part-time undergraduates and 26 semi-structured face-to-face interviews with staff. I visited each case study site as an outsider, a stranger. Nevertheless, as an academic studying an aspect of UK HE; a previous employee within the sector and as a past and present student, I was familiar with the generic features of campus geography: library, lecture theatre, Students' Union and sports facilities, and I was therefore also, to an extent, an insider, a Bourdieusian fish in water, my habitus in alignment with the field. I was both in and of 'the locus of class reproduction . . . and the embodied construction of sociospatial order' (Bridge 2004, p. 63), bringing my own understanding of 'the game' played by students and staff.

> In situations strongly familiar to us, strangeness is not a given but something researchers can only achieve by finding the proper strategies to uncover what is not-so-normal . . . in that sense researchers are like fish trying to discover the water that surrounds them.
>
> (de Jong, Kamsteeg and Ybema 2013, p. 168)

Thinking spatially gave me a means of distancing myself from the taken-for-granted or 'normal' spaces of case study institutions. This involved two key research tools: Massey's 'activity space' and mapping.

Activity space

The device of activity space enables a multiscalar analysis of each case study university without detracting from an idiographic emphasis on the particularity of each institution. In Chapter 6, each university is presented within the extended networks of the sector and economy as a single corporate entity and 'on the ground', for example spatial arrangements, campus geographies, culture and character. Considering each case study university as an agent operating within the spatial network of links and activities of the sector employs Massey's conceptualising an 'extroverted place', that is that 'a large proportion of . . . relations, experiences and understandings are constructed on a far larger scale than what we happen to define for that moment as the place itself' (2005, p. 141). This view emphasises the porosity of institutional borders, the way the policy 'centre' of the government and the HE sector reaches into the workings of individual universities (the NSS, for example): the growing financial significance of retention. It draws attention to the way the university is positioned within the stratified UK HE sector and how this influences the students it attracts. Finally, this view takes account of how the university interacts within its locality and regional economy.

Viewing each case study university as a single corporate body, produces rich data in the form of 'organisational stories', the corporate narratives which are those reproduced, formalised and embedded in the university's corporate literature and communications, for example the university website and social media feeds, mission statement and strategy and policy documents. These stories 'stabilise meaning of particular envelopes of space-time' (Massey 1994, p. 5), securing the institution as 'a site of authenticity . . . singular, fixed and unproblematic in its identity' (*ibid.*) They represent an institutional habitus, shortcuts to institutional identity and ideals and, crucially, communicate who 'belongs' within their boundaries. I was particularly interested in how these stories were reflected or contradicted in the case studies' widening participation and retention strategies and in campus spaces. Gaining an understanding of strategy pathways through institutional structures offered a means of uncovering geographies of power operating within the university. In particular, I paid close attention to the strategic positioning of part-time students in the activity space of each institution.

At ground level, my investigations included the estate and spatial arrangements of each campus: 'the specific spaces . . . produced and stabilised by . . . the dominant groups who occupy them' (Valentine 2008, p. 18). What spaces did mature part-time undergraduates occupy on campus? What diasporic dynamics are at work in these spaces? What were the psychosocial dimensions of that occupation and the implications for belonging? The second spatial research tool, mapping, was an essential contributor to this third-level view.

Mapping

I used mapping not in its dominant form, that is representing space 'as something to be crossed and conquered . . . surface and continuous' (Massey 2005, p. 4), but in a way that 'disputes the internal coherence, the singular uniformity to which the classical map lays claim' (Massey 2005, p. 109). Maps commonly tell a single story of territory, boundary, history and ownership. They hold authority over the narrative of a space but often remain silent on the identity or positionality of the mapmaker. Crang maps 'the student experience', demonstrating how dominant ideas of student culture are embedded in the campus:

> a geography of places – the bars and 'student-friendly' pubs where students can meet new people, the halls of residence, the canteens and faculties around which networks of acquaintances can be formed. The student community is stitched together out of these places; it relies on this geography.
>
> (Crang 1998, p. 5)

I used mapping to seek out the borderlands, the spaces between. In this borderland analysis of belonging, the 'map' of HE is a multidimensional landscape of power and inequality in structured social spaces, territories and trajectories of privilege and disadvantage. It cannot be simply mapped 'as something to be crossed and conquered . . . surface and continuous' (Massey 2005, p. 4). Mapping can, instead, unsettle, disrupt and continually reframe our taken-for-granted understanding of a space or place. Consider for example the Situationists' psychogeographical maps of Paris 'examining the emotional and behavioural impact of urban space upon individual consciousness' (Coverley 2010) and Sinclair's passionate interest in unreported, empty and liminal spaces urban development (1997, 2003, 2009, 2015). 'Massey's plural and fluid understanding of space is reflected in the work of psychogeographer and essayist Rebecca Solnit' (Carruthers Thomas 2017, p. 57). Solnit (2010, 2013) reinterprets the atlas not as a series of static maps but as visual, textual and literary forms created by multiple authors and artists, 'a collection of versions of a place, a compendium of perspectives, a snatching out of the infinite ether of potential versions a few that will be made concrete and visible' (Solnit 2010, p. 2), acknowledging space and our relationships with it as in flux.

Can student belonging be mapped? I developed a bespoke mapping activity, titled *Mapping Belonging*, in which I provided mature part-time undergraduate participants with a campus map and different coloured pens and invited them to mark the places on campus where they felt they 'belonged' and places where they 'did not'. The exercise draws on participatory diagramming, a technique widely used in social geography and development studies. The challenge of representing an intangible and potentially emotive phenomenon in a two-dimensional, visual format aimed to disrupt the familiarity of campus spaces.

> Participant-generated visual materials are particularly helpful in exploring the taken-for-granted things in their research participants' lives . . . [it] involves the participants reflecting on their activities in a way that is not usually done; it gives them distance from what they are usually immersed in and allows them to articulate thoughts and feelings that usually remain implicit.
>
> (Rose 2014, p. 27)

Mature part-time undergraduates' lack of familiarity and limited engagement with the wider university campus emerged across all four case studies. As part of the exercise, participants shared results with one another, a space for common experiences, disagreements and a sharing of information about. The value of *Mapping Belonging* was therefore not only in the visual product of the map itself but also in the discussion and reflection resulting from the task.

Authorship

> As part of our research agenda, we fashion these accounts into a prose piece; we transform biographical interview and field notes into a sociological text. This stage of the research process requires complex decision-making.
>
> – Richardson (1997, p. 26)

Just as acknowledging multiple perspectives challenges the authority of the map to tell a single story and stress the importance of 'the maker's own participation and engagement with the cartographic process' (Corner 1999, p. 229), so it troubles academic conventions which lionise a neutral, rational production of reliable knowledge. Writing a borderland analysis challenges some enduring academic conventions: in rejecting the capacity of a singular paradigm or viewpoint to encompass multiple stories, in creating space for dialogue and in leaving space for tensions as well as synergies. Modelling the authorship of the case study accounts on these principles allows for questions to remain and so can 'leave openings for something new' (Massey 2005, p. 107).

Writing the four case study accounts involved much more than ordering data into a coherent report. It involved developing an authorial voice congruent with this borderland analysis, that is with the social, spatial and psychosocial dimensions of belonging. The accounts distil multiple experiences, perspectives and voices acquired over time into a continuous narrative framed by concepts of space and power. Richardson writes, 'I could no longer write in science's omniscient "voice from nowhere". I was mute but I knew I was "somewhere"'(1997, p. 3). My own and the participants' sense of place and belonging is central to each case study account.

Locating myself within the site, I present myself as a newcomer, a visitor, describing impressions and affective connections to readers, inviting them to interpret the institution through my eyes. I play the role of eavesdropper. I show myself wandering, loitering and sitting in cafés, as well as asking questions, following trails and actively seeking out information. I present myself as an observer, albeit one who is able to demonstrate some authority. As each case study progresses, it becomes clear to readers that I am not a casual visitor but one with privileged access to buildings, information and people. As my understanding evolves, I may make tentative judgements and statements. The result is a series of 'serious fictions' (Gregory 1994) interrogating belonging and integrating the theoretical, methodological and experiential within a narrative dynamic. Each case study account is 'a space of loose ends and missing links' (Richardson 1997, p. 12), depicting the provisionality and partiality of my experience as a researcher and of belonging.

Pen portraits

The four case study universities are briefly described below in preparation for the accounts in Chapter 6. In these pen portraits, note the striking decline in part-time student numbers at each institution between 2010 and 2015, reflecting the 'collapse in part-time study' (Hillman 2015); evidence of a sector in flux, 'always under construction, never finished, closed' (Massey 2005, p. 11).

New Ecclesiastical University gained university status in the last decade and has three campuses in the South of England. A growing institution, it describes itself as 'a non-traditional university . . . in a historic setting'. At the date of selection (2013) over 40 per cent of New Ecclesiastical's students were part-time and 60 per cent mature. By 2016, the proportion of part-time students had fallen to 24 per cent.

(HESA 2015)

Northern City University is an ex-polytechnic which gained university status over twenty years ago. It describes itself as a modern university with a long history which celebrates diversity and offers a vibrant learning experience. Northern City has two city-based campuses. At the date of selection, just over 30 per cent of Northern City's students were part-time and over 40 per cent were mature. By 2016, the proportion of part-time students had fallen to 17.5 per cent.

(HESA 2015)

Modern Eastern University is an ex-polytechnic which gained university status nearly twenty years ago. It has three campuses and is one of the largest institutions in its region. It describes itself as 'non-traditional, inclusive and entrepreneurial'. At the date of selection, like New Ecclesiastical over 40 per cent of Modern Eastern's students were part-time and over 60 per cent were mature. By 2016, the proportion of part-time students had fallen to 22 per cent.

(HESA 2015)

Metropolitan Elite University is a member of the Russell Group of UK research-intensive universities. It describes itself as a multicultural, international institution, accessible to all who have the potential. It has one city-based campus and employs a bespoke model for part-time provision. At the date of selection, 12 per cent of Metropolitan Elite's students were part-time and 25 per cent were mature. By 2016, the proportion of part-time students had fallen to 4 per cent.

(HESA 2015)

References

Abes, L., 2009. Theoretical borderlands: Using multiple theoretical perspectives to challenge inequitable power structures in student development theory. *Journal of College Student Development*, 50 (2), 141–156.

Bridge, G., 2004. Bourdieu. *In*: Hubbard, P., Kitchin, R. and Valentine, G., eds. *Key thinkers on space and place*. London: Sage, 63.

Bryman, A., 2004. *Social research methods*. Oxford: Oxford University Press.

Carruthers Thomas, K., 2017. Towards a Methodology: Organisational Cartographies. *International Journal of Professional Management*, 12 (3), 55–64.

Corner, J., 1999. The agency of mapping: Speculation, critique and invention. *In*: Cosgrove, D., ed. *Mappings*. London: Reaktion, 213–252.

Coverley, M., 2010. *Psychogeography: Pocket essentials*. Harpenden: Pocket Essentials.

Crang, M., 1998. *Cultural geography*. London: Routledge.

Creswell, J.W., 2007. *Qualitative inquiry and research design: Choosing among five approaches*. Thousand Oaks: Sage.

de Jong, M., Kamsteeg, F. and Ybema, S., 2013. Ethnographic strategies for making the familiar strange: Struggling with 'distance' and 'immersion' among Moroccan-Dutch students. *Journal of Business Anthropology*, 2 (2), 168–186.

Geertz, C., 1993. *The interpretation of cultures: Selected essays*. London: Fontana.

Gregory, D., 1994. *Geographical imaginations*. Oxford: Basil Blackwell.

HESA, 2015. Table 6b: *Part-time students by subject, level, sex, age, disability and ethnicity* [online]. Available from: www.hesa.ac.uk [Accessed 4 July 2015].

Hillman, N., ed., 2015. *It's the finance, stupid! The decline of part-time higher education and what to do about it*. London: HEPI.

Massey, D., 1993. Power geometry and a progressive sense of place. *In*: Bird, J., Curtis, B., Putnam, T. and Tickner, L., eds. *Mapping the futures: Local cultures, global change*. London: Routledge, 60–70.

Massey, D., 1994. *Space, place and gender*. Cambridge: Polity Press.

Massey, D., 2005. *For space*. London: Sage.

Merriam, S., 1991. *Case study research in education: A qualitative approach*. San Francisco, CA: Jossey-Bass.

Richardson, L., 1997. *Fields of play: Constructing an academic life*. New Brunswick, NJ: Rutgers University Press.

Rose, G., 2014. On the relation between 'visual research methods' and contemporary visual culture. *The Sociological Review*, 62, 24–46.

Sinclair, I., 1997. *Lights out for the territory*. Cambridge: Granta Books.

Sinclair, I., 2003. *London orbital*. London: Penguin Books.

Sinclair, I., 2009. *Hackney, that rose-red empire*. London: Hamish Hamilton.

Sinclair, I., 2015. *London overground: A day's walk around the ginger line*. London: Hamish Hamilton.

Solnit, R., 2010. *Infinite city*. Berkeley: University of California Press.

Solnit, R., 2013. *Unfathomable city*. Berkeley: University of California Press.

Stake, R., 1994. Case studies. *In*: Denzin, N. and Lincoln, Y., eds. *Handbook of qualitative research*. Thousand Oaks: Sage, 236–247.

Stake, R., 1995. *The art of case study research*. Thousand Oaks: Sage.

Thomas, K., 2016. *Dimensions of belonging: Rethinking retention for mature part-time undergraduates in English higher education* (Unpublished doctoral dissertation). Birkbeck, University of London, London, UK.

Valentine, G., 2008. Living with difference: Reflections on geographies of encounter. *Progress in Human Geography*, 32, 321–335. *In*: Denzin, N. and Lincoln, Y., eds. *Handbook of qualitative research*. Thousand Oaks: Sage, 236–247.

Yin, R.K., 1994. *Case study research: Design and methods*. 2nd ed. Thousand Oaks: Sage.

6 A simultaneity of stories-so-far

Introduction

Abes's argument for working with contradictory perspectives, 'all are viable perspectives that simultaneously describe the complexities of development' (2009, p. 150), is in alignment with Massey's understanding of 'space as a simultaneity of stories-so-far and places as collections of those stories'. (Massey 2005, p. 130). This chapter now presents a simultaneity of stories-so-far selected from the original case study accounts of New Ecclesiastical, Northern City, Modern Eastern and Metropolitan Elite. The stories are voiced by multiple storytellers recounting multiple versions of the university and of belonging. 'Loose ends and ongoing stories are real challenges to cartography' (*ibid.*, p. 107), but I have imposed a thematic map on them to illustrate particular aspects of the theoretical borderlands among Bourdieu, Brah and Massey. Each thematic section begins with an Author's Note and can be read in any order.

Scene setting

Author's note

Each of the following extracts appears at, or very close to the start of, individual case study accounts. They set the scene of the university, its character and its locale. The descriptions capture not only visual and spatial features but also a socio-spatial sense of place as I, the researcher, experienced it. The extracts introduce the idea of the universities as individual activity spaces and as agents within the stratified activity space of the sector: differently positioned, buffeted by politics, policy and funding in continuous flux. They tell stories of the university interacting within urban, economic and historical landscapes. Even in these short extracts, complexity is evident. Expanding campus geographies, evolving university identities, diverse student populations, all place the possibility of a universal and uniform idea of 'belonging in HE' in doubt.

New Ecclesiastical

It's not yet ten o'clock and City campus is quiet; the city centre feels a world, rather than five minutes, away. Low-rise buildings are arranged in a series of interconnecting courtyards with small green spaces, cloistered and contained. A contemporary chapel spire dominates the modest campus skyline. A senior faculty staff member says, 'This campus has a lovely feel. It's very cosy. When people come for open days they immediately feel it would be easy to belong here. It doesn't get much nicer than this'. In the library it's airy, light and open-plan, with small clusters of PCs, group working spaces, sofas and stools in pink, orange, purple and red. Students move the furniture around to suit their needs, creating bespoke study habitats, taking control of the space. If IKEA designed a library, it would be like this.

Different functions – teaching and learning, administration, the library, and student services and student social life – are located on three separate sites, a ten-minute walk apart, meaning that New Ecclesiastical's students and staff constantly cross the city's spaces to learn, work, eat, drink, play and sleep. In fact, the activity space of New Ecclesiastical is intimately bound to its host city. It plays the role of friendly occupier, energetically publicising the financial benefits and opportunities it brings both to the city and the region, not least to disadvantaged communities as well as to its graduates. As student numbers continue to grow, the university is incrementally and opportunistically extending its reach within the limited space, acquiring land and property in the city centre and building new student residences and facilities in order to meet the demands not only of a growing student population but also those students' expectations of 'the traditional, expected, undergraduate experience'. Indicating her office in a glassy new build, a senior executive says, 'We wanted an iconic space here in the city. This building gives us that presence; it's got the wow factor'.

The evolution of New Ecclesiastical from a small teacher-training college to a mid-sized, multi-campus, modern university is part of a wider story of massification and widening participation in English HE. New Ecclesiastical occupies the edges of the HE field, a newcomer to the university club, not just in relation to England's ancient and red-brick institutions but also in comparison with the first post-1992 universities. As the university's identity has evolved, its student cohorts have diversified and its campus network has grown. It currently operates on four campus sites: City, Urban, Coastal and Country, City being the largest and acknowledged as the 'main' campus.

Northern City

It's impossible to miss Northern City's central campus, a complex of over-sized Lego blocks looming above the railway station, badged with a distinctive two-tone logo. The university's buildings stretch out along a busy city street in both directions, spilling into the long, narrow streets of the old industrial centre and, less visibly, occupying whole blocks of the sloping grid between the city centre and the railway line. Cranes signal new builds in progress.

Northern City's history reflects the shifting geometry of social and power relations in the city in which it is located and in the evolving HE sector of which it is a part. Like many 'new' universities, Northern City is an ex-polytechnic, its current incarnation the result of multiple mergers and acquisitions forming one of England's larger universities, in numbers if not in physical estate. The institution's technical and professional past shapes its contemporary identity. 'We have a proud heritage around practical education . . . there's a real emphasis on academic challenge but proximity to practice', says a senior executive. These articulations of past and present versions of Northern City attempt to 'tame' space as temporal, 'always under construction . . . never finished, never closed' (2005, p. 11) but oversimplify the complex positioning of Northern City in the stratified landscape of English HE. 'We do have research and we have some outstanding research but it's in clearly defined areas', says the senior executive. 'We are an institution with teaching at its heart and that's what defines who we are and what we do', he says.

He has genuine concerns about the emphasis on scores and surveys within the sector:

> Maybe we have to capture what it is that students are saying about their experience, as well as looking at the performance numbers, and I don't think we do that as effectively as we might. . . . The NSS is quite a crude instrument, but as a senior manager I have to say it's what matters. It's defining for our league table position.

Modern Eastern

The brick building which fronts Modern Eastern's Central campus is located on a side street close to the city centre. A large glass awning adorns the entrance, an impression of modernity and spaciousness at odds with the interior, which feels slightly dated and definitely cramped. The university bookshop has outgrown its modest floor space; textbooks are piled on the floor like boxes of washing powder in a cut-price supermarket. The thoroughfare between the entrance and the other campus buildings is busy, and above the general hubbub I can hear the ubiquitous soundtrack of university communal spaces – the sound of milk being frothed for coffee.

Modern Eastern's student intake is primarily regional, although the cost of degree study and efficient transport links mean regional boundaries are stretching. An increasing number commute from ever greater distances. The university's popularity – and its appeal to international students – is bound up with the pull of the city as a diaspora space; its adept and profitable fusion of heritage and tech, green space and retail; and its energetic pursuit of new forms of global capital. 'We're on a landlocked site at this campus', the senior executive tells me. 'There's very little room to expand. We've had offers to move out . . . but the students like being in the city; they don't want to be in a field somewhere outside'.

Modern Eastern is constantly adapting to its changing environment. Its dispersed activity space now extends beyond the physical constraints of its three campuses: Central, River and North. The university operates a number of franchises elsewhere in the UK and overseas, delivers online distance learning and serves the training requirements of multiple agencies through its health, social care and education programmes, among others.

Metropolitan Elite

The university sits adjacent to the grey hulk of the city hospital, two pillars of a civilised society occupying a vantage point above the considerable grandeur of this city's centre. Of the city but not in the city. The campus is vast, largely pedestrianised, and bounded by car parks and grid-referenced campus maps announcing, 'YOU ARE HERE'. Its buildings tell stories of patronage and influence, of architectural history: Art Deco Portland stone cheek by jowl with red-brick elegance and blocky modern structures. At nine-thirty on a Monday morning, the rain adds purpose to people's stride. I have an appointment in a contemporary addition to the university estate: an airy, angular building near the campus's eastern edge. It's a few minutes' walk from a busy street along which buses run and where a line of shops and cafés service a constant appetite for coffee, crisps and sandwiches. Some, though by no means all, of Metropolitan Elite's part-time mature students are based in this building, close enough to the edge of campus to find without getting lost in the maze.

In the arena of English HE, Metropolitan Elite is an elite athlete, performing well against national and global competition and attracting investment: a valuable brand. Rooted in the wealth of the city fathers, Metropolitan Elite has no shortage of applications for its degree programmes, despite entry requirements in the upper echelons of the UCAS tariff. It performs strongly in the league tables that matter: student satisfaction, degree outcomes and graduate employment. Not untypically for a Russell Group institution, Metropolitan Elite has high retention rates.

Outwardly unremarkable, the Hub occupies an upper floor of that airy, angular building; it comprises a large, open-plan office; a suite of small private offices; and a kitchen surrounding a modest windowless space. One wall of the central space is taken up with a bank of PCs; another, with noticeboards and bookshelves. There are some tables and chairs, a few sofas and, in one corner, a small children's play area with a bulging toybox. Throughout the interviews this space is regularly referred to as 'a welcoming space', 'a nurturing space', 'a safe haven' and 'a home'.

Geographies of power

Author's note

The following extracts focus on geographies of power operating within and through the activity spaces of the university, how these are sustained and how part-time undergraduates (and other 'non-traditional' students) are positioned as peripheral. University buildings and campus geographies reflect material power; internal geographies of power are detectable in accounts of organisational structures, strategy implementation and the centrality of the full-time, young undergraduate to university business. A Bourdieusian field analysis of HE as a structured social space emerges through stories the universities tell about themselves, part of a positioning process through which they map and protect distinct locations in a 'hierarchy of more/less valued HE' (Bathmaker *et al.* 2008). Organisational stories are reproduced, formalised and embedded in corporate literature and communications such as the university website, social media feeds, branding, mission statements and policy documents. They also emerge in interviews with staff, particularly those in senior and strategic implementation roles, whose responsibility it is to offer a coherent, abstracted organisational picture, literally a view from above. Such stories explicitly or implicitly convey 'who belongs', but the lived experience of students and staff may tell different stories.

New Ecclesiastical

Over the course of my visits, I come to think of the glassy building 'with the wow factor' as the real centre of power at New Ecclesiastical, its command and control centre. Although multifunctional and used by students, the higher floors of the building are closed off to them, and it is here that the policies, regulations, targets and monitoring performed by external bodies, including the government and its proxies, are absorbed and interpreted, implemented and devolved. An intricate geometry of power lines, pulses and currents reach from the outside in and drive internal priorities, strategy and practice, including those in relation to retention.

What happens next? In theory, strategy is disseminated from the centre through a hierarchical network extending across the City campus and to the three satellite campuses, from the executive into faculties and services, from faculty and service executives to departments and from departments to programmes. I interview the institutional lead about retention. 'There was a broad consultation that went through delivery groups, working groups, committees, boards . . . it had the full range'. But then he tells a story of disrupted power lines:

> Once you've got a strategy, then the question you're really asking is, how does it find its way out? If it isn't put in front of people in some forum where it's given some gravitas or incentive, then nobody chooses to go browsing around our strategies.

I follow the trail deeper into the institution, interviewing a faculty executive: 'Whatever the university does at university level, at the moment there's no way of it filtering down into all the faculties'. A member of the academic staff in a different faculty articulates the challenge of implementing wider departmental responsibilities beyond his programme role: 'It's partly my job to disseminate these things, but it's difficult to disseminate stuff and get strategies going if everyone's so busy'.

'City Campus is definitely seen as the main hub. City students probably think of it as the only campus. It's very unlikely they've visited the other campuses', the Student Union manager tells me. 'Coastal is tailored towards younger students, and is very difficult to cater for because they're asking for the same experience as in City, which is impossible'. The senior executive agrees: 'Satisfaction levels in the NSS are not as high at Coastal. The students are much more vociferous about wanting a comparable experience to what they've got here at City'.

The senior executive tells me, 'It's in the lifeblood of this institution to recruit mature and part-time students'. But mature part-time students, occupying significant space in the institution's sense of itself, are currently shrinking in number, occupying only a small percentage of campus space. 'Our partnerships with education and health sectors, among others, have made us vulnerable in a climate of higher fees and declining employer sponsorship', she continues. 'We're not out of line with the sector, in fact we're doing slightly better, but it's extremely hard in the part-time market'.

New Ecclesiastical's retention rate for mature part-time undergraduates is good. The senior executive nods. 'There's not a lot specifically targeted on that group at a central level. . . . We haven't had particular issues around mature students or . . . part-time students with retention'. In fact, their presence in the university's retention strategy document is negligible: the phrase 'part-time' occurs once; the word *mature*, not at all.

> Arrival and orientation is a problematic area for them. Very often they tend to miss out. I'm sure they're invited, but we don't make anything special for them and I think very many of them don't really engage in these sorts of events. I think for part-time students the whole business of getting going is really quite problematic and it's a bit hit and miss. I would guess that they're almost always on the back foot in a way, and that's made up for by the care and attention from the programme staff.

Northern City

Northern City is the 'local' university of the city region, working in partnership with schools and colleges to maintain its localised recruitment. A faculty head says that

> 85 per cent of our natural body of applicants come from within a fifty-mile geographical area and the vast majority . . . are first generation, quite a lot of working class, quite a lot of free school meals, you know, non-standard schools and colleges. I mean that is our natural set of students; it isn't a challenge for us to do that.

A senior executive says, 'We are a very proud widening participation institution. Lots of part-time students, lots of mature students, quite a high proportion of students with disabilities'.

An engagement officer tells me, 'So much is about markets and money now. . . . I don't think universities generally think about part-time provision because they don't think it's where the money is'. The senior executive is more circumspect:

> Part-time is contracting slightly for us now. In terms of the future of the university, we haven't put enough attention on part-time; I think we've lost some of that. But I think there's a realisation that we can't always rely on that traditional full-time undergraduate. . . . I think we will come round to how we can make sure we promote part-time study. And of course we're going to be looking to attract more international students.

Modern Eastern

Like a missile locked onto a target, Modern Eastern's internal geographies of power are driven by sector agendas and power plays, by Massey's 'slices of time' concretised in statistical reports, audits and rankings. 'We're not as far up the league tables as we want to be, although we've been making progress', says a senior executive. 'I have to say, every living hour is devoted in some way or other, not to the National Student Survey *per se*, but to the factors that seem to cause difficulties'.

A services director tells me, 'We're very transparent. We talk to each other. There's a down side to that: we spend a lot of time in meetings but we don't do things without a consensus'. She cites the development of a new corporate plan. 'About 120 people worked at it together, trapped in a room with each other for two days'. Here, then, is a key node of the geography of power at Modern Eastern, no doubt with its own hierarchies among that large group of senior staff.

'Those of us who choose to teach adult classes . . . do set up a kind of protective enclave for them', says a lecturer.

> We try to make the hours better; we try to get them in a decent room and keep the room; we try to nurture; we try to plan the sessions around their needs. Massification, to use that horrible nominalisation, is making increasingly difficult to put that little bit extra in. Timetabling is quite centralised and quite tight. It has to be. I understand the reasons. So if you've got a room booked for two hours . . . you'll have another class in immediately after you. It's very difficult to talk to students afterwards. Everyone is rushing off and rushing in.

She tries to compensate in the classroom:

> I squeeze some of the teaching where the work-related content is more easily accessible to them, and put more time into 'how are you going to structure an essay?' 'How are you going to do this referencing?' But if our timetabling is up against the various increases . . . any nurturing you do on top of that timetabled two hours is actually extra teaching and I think that's an issue too.

Academic staff on the frontline, it becomes a familiar theme.

Metropolitan Elite

The existence of the Hub is the result of restructuring driven by twin forces: the shape-shifting of lifelong learning and part-time HE within the sector and OFFA's requirement for those universities charging more than £6,000 a year in tuition fees to spell out their provision for under-represented groups. A senior manager in the Hub tells me,

> The deal for us within this research intensive university is to support the university's diversification of its student body. One of the ways the university chooses to do that for mature and part-time learners is to have a unit like ours, which has them at its heart. The university as a whole is very big, big enough to be a city in its own right . . . we try to be a village within it.

So the Hub is both separate *and* integrated? 'We determine our own terms of entry . . . we make our own internal decisions as long as we're in line with university strategy'. The Hub is one semi-autonomous universe within another: Metropolitan Elite.

Belonging in HE (on paper)

Author's note

The following extracts reflect ways in which the narrative of student belonging becomes embedded in institutional strategy, policies and practices. Universities invest in it, in social learning spaces, clothing, merchandise and schemes, but a blanket rhetoric often conceals peripheral student identities and ways of engaging with the university. Staff pragmatically acknowledge the plurality and partiality of attachments. Spaces open between rhetoric and lived experience.

New Ecclesiastical

The university's retention strategy adopts, wholesale, the discourse of belonging articulated in *What Works?* (2012) to the extent of prefacing its strategy objectives and action plan with direct quotes from the report: 'A sense of belonging in HE significantly informs a student's subsequent decisions to stay and then to succeed. The first year of a programme needs to be designed to promote this' (*ibid.*).

But an inconsistency emerges between the single story of retention and belonging in the strategy and staff members' perceptions of belonging as it applies to mature part-time students. The senior executive tells me: 'It's been shown its got the greatest impact on retention if students get this sense of belonging, but . . . it may not be something that particularly applies to part-time mature undergraduates who don't have so much of that sense of

I need to feel I am part of this and so on. With part-time, it's how do you keep the motivation for their wanting to continue to engage in this level of study when they've got their domestic arrangements, their family arrangements, if they're working full-time at the same time?' An academic colleague agrees:

> We're just something they do, like doing a yoga class on Thursday night . . . belonging doesn't really work for them. The issue is more to do with how they can fit their professional lives into what we do, how they can find space and time. Part-time students are almost always on the back foot in a way, and that's made up for by the care and attention from the programme staff.

A member of staff responsible for enrichment activities comments,

> Engaging in the extra-curricular stuff is quite hard for students with childcare, or a job, or who don't live close to the university. But if you've got an established life and established identity, maybe it's not so upsetting if you don't feel that involved?

Northern City

There are no longer university statements about widening participation. The rhetoric has changed to reflect changes to regulatory mechanisms – and funding sources. 'The discussion is fair access, but fair access is not a problem here', says a faculty head. A partnerships executive explains:

> We've moved away from a discrete widening participation agenda towards inclusion . . . as an organisation we put emphasis on having an inclusive approach to students, to learning and support . . . rather than focusing on a particular target audience and supporting them in a particular way.

He adds,

> It's not that there aren't differences between all kinds of students in different groups in different ways, but our philosophy extends across the entire student population. If we adopt an inclusive approach to students, you are trying to create a sense in which they belong.

'What's come through our strategy development is the importance of belonging, identity, or a sense of affiliation for students with their course of study', says a senior executive. 'It seems to be that when students feel a strong sense of affiliation with their course, not only do they experience higher levels of satisfaction . . . but they seem to do better, they progress, they attain better'. He enthuses about the development of spaces in which staff and students can work together on their subject. 'It's about that proximity . . . about students almost becoming part of that community of practice, from day one'. Northern City has developed a set of social learning hubs: common, informal, multipurpose spaces in departmental buildings. One such space is the Glasshouse, a five-storey, glass-roofed communal space at City campus. A senior executive enthuses,

> The Glasshouse not only links what were quite disparate buildings on the campus . . . it's created a heart, a genuinely democratic space. An extension of the office, the classroom, the lab; an extension of the learning and working space. A feeling that I belong there as much as you do, as much as you do.

Modern Eastern

A faculty lead leans forward and points to a small badge on his lapel.

> You'll see I'm wearing an *I 'heart' Modern Eastern* badge. This is a campaign . . . to try and increase the sense of community here. On certain days, if you're wearing something that's university-badged or branded clothing, you'll get a free tea or coffee. It's to try and increase the visible triggers of belonging.

All new students at Modern Eastern receive a branded T-shirt free of charge. 'It's organic cotton', a professional services executive tells me. 'What we really want is people wearing their pride and to go off campus with their stuff on and ideally to wear it on other days'. She suggests the free-drink scheme can benefit coffee drinkers and part-time mature students alike. 'If when you come onto campus you're wearing branded stuff and you see others doing the same . . . you could feel you were taking part . . . it's a small thing about belonging'.

The faculty lead says,

> All universities try and socialise their students into becoming 'university students', but if they're not on campus, how can we do it? If they're still here after six weeks, they're probably here for good. Especially if they're still here after the first set of assessments. But if they haven't found a space for themselves in the first six weeks, they're likely to go.

Metropolitan Elite

The Hub's senior director says,

> For many of our students their initial assumptions would be that the university is a relatively hostile place or one that isn't likely to regard them very highly. . . . I think they come to realise that that picture of the university is . . . a bit simplistic. . . . I think they come to feel they belong in it because they know they belong somewhere in it. For our part-time students especially, we've had to acknowledge that their primary place of belonging is their course and, perhaps secondarily, this Hub, you can't have one without the other. And within all that, a sort of sense of the university. Retention is a greater challenge for us. It's to do with the whole mix of circumstances within which our learners are working . . . the whole business of juggling lives that are already much more committed than those of younger learners typically. That also unites with a fairly frequent phenomenon, which is that adult returners typically are not always confident about their capabilities in relation to HE.

In response, the Hub has developed its own detailed Retention Strategy and Action Plan, which imagines retention as a longitudinal, multifaceted project. Its wraparound support services – finance, welfare and careers development – are available to all mature and part-time students across the university throughout their student journey.

Doing HE differently

Author's note

The following set of stories explore how the nature and demands of part-time study and maturity shape the way students engage with HE and have implications for the ways in which they inhabit and claim campus space. Often clustered in vocational and professional degree programmes, many of this study's undergraduate participants are taught in homogenous cohorts with particular temporal characteristics: 'the Wednesday evening group', 'Saturday students'. Although this perpetuates peripherality from the student 'norm', part-time undergraduates' complex everyday routines are commonplace within their classrooms. There are also examples of the physical, social and virtual dimensions of the learning environment becoming sites of shared understandings between student and staff members who themselves experience a sense of difference and peripherality in a system geared towards full-time study.

New Ecclesiastical

Multiple professional and personal commitments shape students' interaction with the campus. The amount of time they have to spend *on* campus limits the spaces they occupy *in* it. 'Placement rips people out for vast swathes of time', observes a senior manager.

> And at Urban, we know even if they're full time, let's say on the Health programmes, they only hit the campus when they have to, and then they're off. Part-time students can't just drift in. They tend to be based off-site and not hang around. There's a real difference between our students at Coastal campus wanting to be a New Ecclesiastical student and wear the sweatshirt and our students at Urban campus. At Urban they know why they're there. They're not doing this just for HE . . . they have a very definite target.

One student at Urban sums up her 'student experience': 'It's every Monday, five sessions per module, six modules, thirty Mondays'. A programme director tells me, 'Even at City, when part-time students come in they're probably only here for actual contact time, and there's that thing, parking, and there isn't time to go to the library and back again'. Even the ten- to fifteen-minute walk between the City campus sites suddenly seems a real inconvenience in an inflexible schedule.

Another programme director says, 'I've been invited onto a couple of review panels and, as somebody described it, *Oh you're here to talk about the odd programmes*'. This attitude seems incongruous in a young university like New Ecclesiastical, with its ethos of inclusion. It's as if the newer models of the academy cannot escape a traditional institutional habitus.

> The battles I have as programme director with the university through central services are still trying to explain that our students don't follow a traditional academic year or an official university day . . . we do feel we're banging our head against a brick wall. Why are we still doing that?

The Students' Union manager acknowledges the emphasis is on activities which appeal to young, full-time, home students:

> The sort of services and events we offer seem to drift towards young people who only have their degree to do at this moment in time. Those things don't appeal to mature students, and part-time students are very likely to miss them. We do want them to have a New Ecclesiastical identity, but . . . we do tend to forget a bit about them. The sabbatical

officers tend to be young, full-time students, so it's difficult for them to understand the issues. When you get a part-time or mature student to run for any leadership position, you definitely put them on the map. Then that thinking starts getting implemented. The difficulty is to make them run to begin with.

Northern City

Student B says, 'This is somewhere you come every couple of weeks, then go. We come on a Saturday so everything's shut. It's like a ghost town. You're lucky if you can get a cup of coffee or a warm drink'. Student C is also a Saturday student. 'We're the only people here on a Saturday. We all give up our weekends to be able to study. Everybody's sort of in the same boat'. She adds, 'In terms of the university I've not had a great deal to do with it to be honest. I don't think I've got time as a part-time student. I work 45 hours a week, plus coming to university at weekends'.

'My students are operating as leaders or managers; they've got a lot going on at work that encroaches on home life, as well as study', says a lecturer who runs a part-time degree for health-service professionals.

> For some it's just not possible to balance it, and I think the support they get from their organisation varies. Some have protected time, some don't; some are using holidays or days off to work round it. And there's always lots of restructuring and job changes, promotions – a lot of variables that play for them. I think the thing is they need to be able to plan, almost to the minute. I'm not aware that my part-time students participate in anything other than what has to be done on that day. And I've not heard any speak about social events of social life within the university.

A lecturer on a part-time programme says her students have developed their own Facebook group. 'They need quick sources of information and support. Facebook is more synchronous than the VLE; they don't really engage with the VLE'. A final-year part-time student who created a Facebook page for her year group tells me, 'It's probably used as the go-to support over other streams of support. Facebook is so instantaneous. It's well used. No tutors allowed, because we use it as a sounding board as well' She adds, 'Our tutors will do Skype, they'll do email, they'll do late night tutorials if that's what we need. . . . The tutors are really supportive, it's just the wider university system is not geared up for part-time students'.

'No matter what we do with our space so that our full-time students can really have that sense of belonging, how does that translate for those students who come on to the campus at different times?' muses a senior executive.

I think that's a real challenge. If you're on campus in the evening most of the catering outlets, if not all, are closed after 6pm and there is very little going on, although the Learning Centre is open. So places feel dark and empty.

Another manager agrees:

I'm absolutely sure there's stuff that could be done . . . to create, enhance or strengthen that sense of 'belonging' for part-time and mature students, but if you're geared predominantly to full-time undergraduate students, then your estate is geared up for that. . . . As an institution, you may want to shift to accommodate the needs and issues of other groups of students, but the logistics and costs are quite difficult.

Modern Eastern

A faculty head says,

The vast majority of our students are full-time, but they're full-time in name only. The vast majority work up to the limit of what is allowed, and I dare say some exceed it. Every student's part-time now, yet we are continuing to treat them like full-time students.

He identifies a general trend away from what he describes as 'fully committing'.

Limited part-time student hours combined with lecturers delivering programmes across university campuses can cause problems with the personal tutoring system, as one student participant explains: 'We're only in one day a week, we have lectures nine to four. So if our lecturers are only in on that day, we're supposed to get extra support when?' Another tells me,

We do have a personal tutor, we just don't have a lot of contact with them. It comes down to time, and when we're in the university and when they're in the university. Time isn't built into our programme for appointments. We have to sacrifice time. And that's not practical, because we're already asking a lot of our employers.

'For our students', says a course leader at Modern Eastern's North campus,

university life is that day when they're in. They want tutorials on that day, so the days are manic because you've got them queueing up. As well as emotional support, what we offer is that much more intensive support because we've got smaller groups and we reach them quicker. This year I make sure I go into the café on the days they're in and go round and say hello and have a chat. It normally means I don't end up actually eating if I'm teaching afterwards . . . but at least it's communication.

I ask her what it's like from a staff perspective, to be sited at North campus. 'It's taken a lot of time for us to feel part of the wider picture, but one has to be persistent. . . . I think we do get isolated; we are slightly the forgotten outpost. It's always, *oh – and North campus*'. The distance from decision-making centres and the relatively smaller size of both campus and cohort are compounded by the part-time nature of her programme.

I'm always in there with elbows, fighting for part-time. We're not a big cohort here, and a lot of the decisions are made on the full-time and the Masters and I have to say – *have you thought about part-time*? You have to be quite assertive! Our library is not as big as the other campus libraries, the students moan there aren't enough books. We can't offer the students a *let's stay on campus have a riot life*.

Metropolitan Elite

One student participant, a younger male, describes his first year of study as like playing Russian roulette. 'I've spent most of the semesters juggling two part-time jobs and trying to find work for the holidays. Even without kids, it can be very difficult'. I ask a lecturer whether part-time study presents structural obstacles to belonging beyond the cohort. 'Certainly the part-time students treat university as a part-time evening class', says a lecturer. 'They have their jobs and then, for example on a Wednesday night . . . they come here for three hours, they study and then they return to their lives until next week'.

Hub staff stress that, in fact, part-time and mature undergraduates are dispersed unevenly across the university as a whole. 'It's just that the Hub is the specialist provider. We were designed . . . to be quite an unusual centre, a hybrid of a school and a service', says a student support officer. He acknowledges that their specialised remit can create problems. 'People (in faculties) are not intentionally bad at supporting mature students . . . but there's work to do on educating people how they *can* support them rather than palming them off on us'. 'I think at this institution it's the right model', the unit's director tells me. 'Part-time students would very easily get lost within the faculties if they didn't have some way of being championed or having a centre like this to advocate their needs'.

I recall a conversation I had with a member of staff in the unit. She told me that some part-time and mature undergraduates, most living locally, start their university studies a week ahead of Freshers Week, with a gentle intro- duction to the campus. The students are encouraged to find their feet, to explore, but, having tentatively begun to do so, Freshers' Week arrives and the campus is suddenly invaded by 'hordes of young, triple-A students'. Feeling outnumbered and displaced, the part-timers retreat to the safety of the Hub. It's a diasporic dynamic with a reverse twist: the minority of locals positioned by majority 'migrants' who effortlessly claim a better cultural fit with the spaces of the university. I think of the maps dotted around the campus, the arrow confirming that 'YOU ARE HERE'. Young full-time students can be in no doubt that they 'belong' at Metropolitan Elite.

Mapping belonging

Author's note

Across all four case studies, mature part-time undergraduates' maps of belonging and the accompanying discussions, reveal limited engagement with the campus beyond the classroom. Participants' enthusiasm and appre- ciation for higher-level learning are overlaid with discomfort about age differences and a lack of confidence and 'fit'. There is negligible engage- ment with the familiars of contemporary 'student life' – the Students' Union building, the bar, the gym. For many, quiet buildings, distant satellites, closed cafés and empty vending machines are the more familiar experiences of institutional spaces.

New Ecclesiastical

I give out campus maps and coloured pens to a group of first-year mature part-time undergraduates at Urban campus. I ask them to indicate with dif- ferent colours the places on campus where they feel they 'belong' and those places where they don't. We use the terms *hot spots* and *cold spots* as a shorthand. One stares at the map and then exclaims, 'Is it that big? I've only ever been in two buildings on this campus. Are we allowed in that sports hall?' The 'hot spots' are limited to the classroom and the library. A student with an hour-long commute to campus comments, 'The only thing I've seen is the train station and my walk here from the bus stop'. Another shrugs, 'I've got so much stuff needs doing at home, why would I want to spend any more time here than I need to?'

I run another Student Workshop at City campus. The students are taught in a satellite building some miles away from the main campus. It takes ten minutes by car on a fast road to reach the building, a bland, modern, multipurpose centre badged with the university logo. I give the students a City campus map, but their building doesn't feature on it. Some students draw it on the edge of the sheet of paper; some use arrows to indicate its location. One student rings the entire main campus site in blue. 'I've just said "cold" for the whole thing because I don't even know where it is'. One student says, 'I've been to the library a few times but I think people look at me and think, *Who's that old person over there*?' A female student of a similar age complains,

> I studied for two years at Coastal campus before coming here. I felt so detached; we were just off to the side rather than in the hub and the hustle and bustle. Out here we're kind of on the side as well.

A male student in his 20s says,

> We're only here one day a week; it's difficult to make those bonds. I don't think they've necessarily done anything wrong, but it's just somewhere I come to once a week. We do get emails, like about sports, but you wouldn't go. Imagine turning up and not being part of it!

Northern City

My efforts to arrange Student Workshops with self-selecting mature part-time students at Northern City prove unsuccessful, largely due to their complex and crowded schedules. Two attempts to set up sessions with 'captive' participants in subject groups also fall through. Instead, I conduct three individual interviews with three mature part-time undergraduates (one male – Student A – and two females – Students B and C), snatching half hours in café or lobby spaces as they're on their way to or from lectures and tutorials. Asked to map hot and cold spots of belonging on campus maps, Students B and C highlight the primary building in which they are taught and the Learning Centre. Nothing more. Student C says, 'There's loads of buildings but I don't need to go to them. I know you can get support for accommodation but I don't need it; I've come to university having got my career. I know what I want to do in the future as well'. She has paid only one visit to the Students' Union building. I ask what had it felt like to go in to on that occasion? 'Busy! You're not used to it when you're a Saturday student'. Other than her departmental building and the Learning Centre, Student B's map consists almost entirely of 'cold spots', which she colours in with a green pen.

> I don't feel comfortable in this building. No idea what that is, no idea what's there. Don't know my way around there. I only feel partially

comfortable in the Learning Centre. If you come in the week it's very busy and it feels a bit scary. It's better when it's quiet at weekends. We come on a Saturday so everything's shut. It's like a ghost town. You're lucky if you can get a cup of coffee or a warm drink.

What about the Glasshouse, I ask her. Would you hang out there? 'No, no, no. No belonging in the Glasshouse! I'm not sure it's even open on a Saturday, unless there's an event on?'

Modern Eastern

I run a workshop with mature part-time students on a bespoke part-time programme at North campus. The workshop is squeezed into their lunch hour; participants come and go, munch sandwiches and crisps. I am acutely aware that they are giving up the one time in the day they might be getting fresh air or chatting with friends. During the workshop we discuss their experiences of part-time study. We don't do the *Mapping Belonging* exercise because there is no map of North campus, and they never visit the other campuses. The participants do know about the free-coffee-for-branded-clothing scheme but are less than enthusiastic. When I ask them what they value most about their experience, one says, to general agreement, 'Meeting these guys, the group. It's like camaraderie in the bunker!' Contact with other students, including other year groups in their programme, is almost non-existent, inhibited by timetabling and external commitments. There is no mention of engaging with university societies. 'I think we're the poorer relation', comments one participant. 'City campus is much better equipped. We have to pay the same as they do, but we're never going to be the same'.

Metropolitan Elite

I run two Student Workshops at Metropolitan Elite: one involving fifteen self-selecting mature students from the unit and schools across the university and the other 30 mature part-time undergraduates studying a vocational degree programme, employed locally and attending the university one afternoon a week. Asked to map out the places on campus where they feel a sense of belonging and those where they don't, it becomes clear that excursions into university territory are problematic for some. 'When I go into the big computer clusters, I feel a bit apprehensive that they'll think, *what's the old lady doing here?*' says one. 'I've hardly used the university at all because I live very close. I tend to come in for lectures then go home via the library. I prefer the quiet working environment at home', says another. The

Students' Union building and what it represents inspire a range of responses, mainly indifferent or negative. One student complains,

> Even though I've got disabilities and I'm old and all that, I'm still a bit of a party animal and one thing I've definitely realised is that this is our bit and we don't belong in that bit. We're not accepted anywhere else. You can walk through the Students' Union and they don't even look at you.

A fellow participant nods. 'Yes, they ignore us'.

Dimensions of belonging

Author's note

Asked what they value most about their student experience, many participants cited the camaraderie of fellow students and the way in which their cohort or elements of it provided a long-term support structure, but other, less obvious, factors are also at work. Everyday experiences of mature part-time undergraduates may be less visible to the strategic centre of the university but nevertheless offer multiple opportunities for connection and attachment. Diaspora spaces at the periphery carry the potential for negotiation of new or experimental identities, a re-scripting of everyday lives. Dimensions of belonging are negotiated in the momentary, the imaginary and the private.

New Ecclesiastical

Mature part-time undergraduates are the majority in Nursing, Allied Health and some Education programmes. 'Predominantly more mature women, between 30 and 50 with families . . . relatively few men . . . and relatively few youngsters but we're seeing that gently increase', says a programme manager in Education. I ask him for his view of his mature part-time undergraduates' sense of belonging.

> If you talk about being part of this university – not so much. But there's a strong cohort identity. Usually, the constant is the group and whatever's happening in the group and the variable is the tutor, possibly six different tutors in the year. We tend to see that the cohorts are very supportive of each other, and that fosters that 'belonging' within that group. They want to graduate with their cohort at the cathedral.

'A lot of them are what I'd call women returners', the senior executive explains.

> They want to be a nurse, they want to be a radiographer, they want to be an occupational therapist, they want to be a social worker. They've got a particular identity as largely vocational. They are primarily our population at Urban campus. Their alignment is really with their professional group, their Nursing cohort and so on. And when they go into hospitals they'll be very proud to be wearing their university uniform as trainee health professionals; from that point of view they would see themselves as part of this university.

She argues that for those on vocational degree programmes, alignment with a professional identity compensates for limited temporal and physical engagement with the campus.

Northern City

I ask Student B if she feels like a student? 'No. I feel like a wife and a mother and a businesswoman'. Each of these aspects of her identity motivates her study:

> I want to provide a better life for my family. We live in a very deprived area of the city . . . we know ultimately we're going to have to move house to make sure our daughter has the best possible chance in life. I do feel part of my course; I very much feel part of my year group. You have your own little community within your classroom and, to quote from Bruner's Ecological Systems theory, you've got your little microsystem and your mesosystem.

I ask Student C, 'Do you like wearing a hoodie that says Northern City on it?'. 'Yes', she replies. 'It does give you a sense of belonging: you know, I'm a Northern City student sort of thing . . . it's the excitement that I'm part of the university'. I observe that she's not wearing it today. 'I've had it that long, it's all bobbly and I wear it at home when I do my uni work'. Does Student B own a Northern City hoodie? 'I do', she says.

> I own several and I've had my business name printed on the back! I thought it would help me feel like I belong, but does it really? You see students wearing Northern City stuff and you think – yeah, I'm a student, I deserve one of those. But really . . . it's just making you feel like you blend in that little bit. Because you do look out of place.

Student A has become course rep for his seminar group. The role has, he feels,

> definitely cemented my links to the university. I get a chance to talk to people I wouldn't usually talk to in a normal day's learning. It's nice to be able to sit down and talk to tutors as an adult. And now people external to my course say, *Hello how are you*? and that gives you a nice sense of belonging.

Modern Eastern

'Probably two thirds of our students at River Campus commute', says the faculty lead. 'We don't have so many traditional students there', says the services executive. 'As a result, mature students tend to feel quite at home. It's the transient nature . . . they're either part-time or they're on programmes which include placements'.

One Student Workshop participant says, 'The only reason I'm still here is these people'. She indicates her fellow students. I ask the group what they value most about their experience, another participant says, to general agreement, 'Meeting these guys, the group. It's like camaraderie in the bunker!' A third says,

> It must be an uphill struggle for the tutors who are trying to do the best for everybody. In our experience, our best tutors were both part-time students before they were tutors, so they've lived this journey. But they're also victims of their own success, because they're really good and everybody wants their time because they're the most helpful people. Our tutor last year knew all of us, all of our names, all of our grades . . . if your marks went down she would keep an eye on it and be straight on it.

A lecturer smiles resignedly when she says, 'I think, in a funny way, students get a sense of belonging because they have a shared gripe . . . there's nothing like something going wrong to make a group feel happy!'

Metropolitan Elite

I ask the leader of the Hub's Foundation programme whether mature part-time undergraduates 'belong' at Metropolitan Elite and if so, to what.

> They belong to the mature cohort and the Hub – although the programme they're on is a stronger identity. My students see themselves

as Foundation students without a doubt and they see themselves as being different in the university. And this gives them a sense of belonging.

A diasporic minority creating a home in new a territory, negotiating a sense of belonging from a position of difference?

A couple of Student Workshop participants display some enthusiasm for the Students Union. 'I come in every Saturday morning for my breakfast before I go to the library', says one female participant. 'I know quite a few of the bar staff, they're on my course', says a male participant. Another female participant studying not in the Hub but in one of the university schools mitigates a sense of difference through engaging in extra-curricular activities based in the Union. 'I've really thrown myself into things, I've joined societies and there are a lot of mature students engaged with those societies'. A fellow participant comments, 'I've no time to join societies, I'm working'.

Staying on course can be about what individuals imagine academia might be and what they might become. A male student participant says thoughtfully,

> I feel I belong to my school but not necessarily the university. One reason I like my school is that it gives me a sense of being part of a disciplinary community which is wider than the university. It's an intro-duction into that academic world, if you know what I mean.

A female participant says, 'I've waited all my life to study. I've made sacri-fices to get here. Why would I drop out?' 'I just keep thinking of my hat and gown', says another, smiling. The longer learners remain, the more tantalis-ing is the desired end point: 'You think – you can actually do this. You think, it's within your reach'.

'There isn't much to share because your lifestyle is so different', says a female undergraduate in her late sixties.

> I don't think I expected to fit in. But the young students are always polite, and each year there's always a couple who've been really friendly. And I've made some wonderful friends with other mature students. I brought my grandson in and played snooker on the tables they've got in the Union. It was lovely. I thought, this is *my* university, I can do what I want!

Her words reveal an emotional investment in HE, in the university and in herself.

References

Abes, L., 2009. Theoretical borderlands: Using multiple theoretical perspectives to challenge inequitable power structures in student development theory. *Journal of College Student Development*, 50 (2), 141–156.

Bathmaker, A., Brooks, G., Parry, G. and Smith, D., 2008. Dual-sector further and higher education: policies, organisations and students in transition. *Research papers in education*, 23 (2), 125–137.

Massey, D., 2005. *For space*. London: Sage.

Epilogue

This book challenges a powerful and ubiquitous narrative of student belonging in HE; of belonging as tied to specific activities and forms of engagement on and around campus. It is a narrative which has become tightly entangled in prevailing agendas of student retention, student engagement and the student experience within the UK HE sector. The book maps a theoretical trajectory which began with a Bourdieusian analysis of power and social inequalities and led to a borderland analysis, generating new theoretical territory among Bourdieu, Brah and Massey. I have argued that we can use their ideas of space and power and relationships between them to (re)theorise student belonging as relational, contested, negotiated and in process. This is a particular mapping at a particular time, focusing on mature part-time undergraduates in the UK HE sector, but is transferable to other HE contexts and diverse student constituencies.

This re-imagining of student belonging was triggered by studying the literature of student retention, an encounter 'with the apparently familiar, but where something continues to trouble and unexpected lines of thought slowly unwind' (Massey 2005, p. 6). I sensed that the 'trouble' lies in the substance and significance of spaces between a 'common understanding of what belonging means and why belonging is important' (Mee and Wright 2009, p. 772).

> Despite its ubiquitous nature the concept of belonging remains curiously undertheorised by social scientists . . . perhaps because it is such a taken-for-granted concept. Such commonsense, taken-for-granted phenomena deserve critical analysis because despite their deceptive appearance of being 'natural' they are shaped by social forces.
>
> (May 2009, p. 3)

Full-time study now not only holds the centre ground of English HE; it also crowds the whole territory, pushing different ways of engaging with higher-level study to a strategically precarious periphery. The cultural capital of young, full-time students fuels the engine with which the model reproduces itself over and over. The rules, rhythms and traditions of the traditional university model continue to dominate the field, shaping and governing play. The centre shifts, resets and shifts again, but the essential topography of the territory holds firm, and power relationships still define the periphery. Enduring institutional practices stabilise an exclusive hegemonic student culture, a map of meaning. Yet as our HE system continues to evolve, diversify and become ever more complex, rethinking belonging requires re-imagining relationships between centre and periphery in a way that acknowledges and values spaces between.

I have attempted to rethink belonging between binaries of traditional/ non-traditional, belonging/not-belonging. I have scrutinised campus spaces and their geographies of power, experiencing and eliciting the psychosocial dimension of space. I have tried to understand what is happening between the rhetoric of belonging on the page or the screen and the lived, longitudinal experience of student persistence. I have listened to organisational stories which strain against changes wrought in the sector by successive strategic and policy shifts and lose currency as wider geographies of power in the activity spaces of sector and institution determine criteria for viability and competitiveness. As organisations outgrow established narratives, resistances evolve and spaces open between rhetoric and experience. These spaces become occupied by other stories-so-far. I have listened to those stories too.

In New Ecclesiastical, Northern City, Modern Eastern and Metropolitan Elite I discovered mature part-time undergraduates in distinct and limited spaces: clustered in vocational programmes, in satellite buildings and in fractured cohorts. I discovered a corporate rhetoric of belonging and resistance to it. I learned to look beyond physical boundaries and into the interstices of contested activity spaces for evidence of partial, negotiated and alternative belongings. I discovered diaspora spaces in self-generated Facebook groups, in shared sandwich lunches and professional identities, in Wednesday evening and Saturday student cohorts and in solidarity forged in echoing, depopulated university buildings and in the camaraderie of the bunker.

I found points of attachment in public and private spaces. Participants in all case study universities negotiated dimensions of belonging with their cohorts in the classroom, café or through social media and through shared experiences of the workplace, home or locality. I found dimensions of belonging in the imaginary, momentary and private: the second-year student visualising her graduation 'hat and gown', the young professional who wears a university-branded hoodie when studying at home, the student anticipating membership of a wider academic community, the delight of a grandmother playing snooker with her grandson in 'her' Students' Union building. And I found dimensions of belonging in the localised, intensive relationships mature part-time undergraduates often develop with individual tutors, a sense of shared ownership at the human interface between institution and individual. Whether in isolated pockets of a university or in a departmental framework such as the Hub, all the case studies reveal multiple examples of compensatory behaviour by staff trying to bridge the gaps between a rhetoric of student belonging and complex lived experience. Their efforts are hard to measure and don't figure in institutional rankings, but this is critical work. It takes root in part-time undergraduates' learning, encourages persistence and the development of an evolving sense of a place for themselves in the context of higher-level study.

Abes writes, 'I brought together two different theoretical perspectives not as a blueprint for how this interdisciplinary theoretical work ought to be done, but instead as one possibility' (2009, pp. 143–144). Similarly, this borderland analysis of student belonging is not prescriptive; its purpose is to contribute towards a rethinking of student belonging in a way which might reframe institutional approaches to richly diverse student populations. I say 'towards' deliberately. 'Any effort at definition . . . analytically fixes and mobilises pro and contra positions' (Lather 1991, p. 5). The purpose of this book is to emphasise the rich territory of spaces between, to 'leave openings for something new' (Massey 2005, p. 107). I invite you to re-imagine centre and periphery as common spaces intersected by multiple networks of social relations and universities as multiple centres experienced in multiple ways and belonging as a dimensional phenomenon negotiated in spaces between.

References

Abes, L., 2009. Theoretical borderlands: Using multiple theoretical perspectives to challenge inequitable power structures in student development theory. *Journal of College Student Development*, 50 (2), 141–156.

Lather, P., 1991. *Getting smart: Feminist research and pedagogy with/in the postmodern*. New York: Routledge.

Massey, D., 2005. *For space*. London: Sage.

Mee, K. and Wright, S., 2009. Geographies of belonging. *Environment and Planning A*, 41, 772–779.

Index

Abes, L. 25–28, 42, 47, 57, 83
Action on Access 9
activity space: overview 41–42; as research tool 49–50
Anzaldúa, Gloria 26–27
authorship 52–53

belonging: author's experience of 4; borderlands and 27–28; common understanding of 23; as geographical 5; Maslow on 3; as relational 3, 31–36; as social 3, 36–38
belonging in higher education: changing spaces of higher education and 10–12; engagement and 12–13, 15–16; experiences of 3–4; identification and 37; Metropolitan Elite University 68; Modern Eastern University 67; narrative of 81; New Ecclesiastical University 65–66; Northern City University 66–67; rethinking 5–6, 81–83; sense of, and retention and success 5, 9; in strategy, policies and practices 65; *see also* dimensions of belonging; *Mapping Belonging* activity
Birkbeck, University of London 22
borderland analysis: activity space in 49–50; authorship in 52–53; case study in 48–49; characteristics of 25–27; individual habitus and 31–36; mapping in 50–52; methodology of 47–48; overview 27–28; pen portraits of 53–54; psychosocial dimension of belonging and 36–38; space and power in 42; spatial thinking and 39–42, 47–48

Bourdieu, Pierre 5, 28, 31–36, 38–39
Brah, Avtar 28, 36–38, 39
bricolage, principles of 26

case study method 48–49
class and participation in higher education 19
constructivism 27
Crosland, Antony, speech of 10
cultural capital 32, 34

diagramming, participatory 51
diaspora space 38, 41
diasporic dynamic 36–38, 39
dimensions of belonging: Metropolitan Elite University 78–79; Modern Eastern University 78; negotiation of 82–83; New Ecclesiastical University 76–77; Northern City University 77–78; overview 76
Dimensions of Belonging (Thomas) 1–2
doing higher education differently: Metropolitan Elite University 72–73; Modern Eastern University 71–72; New Ecclesiastical University 69–70; Northern City University 70–71; overview 68

Education Reform Act of 1988 10
engagement and belonging 12–13, 15–16
Equivalent or Lower Qualification (ELQ) ruling 22
ethnicity and participation in higher education 19

feminist geography 40
field 32, 34
field analysis 32, 39, 41

gender and participation in higher
    education 19
geographies of power: Metropolitan
    Elite University 64–65; Modern
    Eastern University 64; New
    Ecclesiastical University 61–63;
    Northern City University 63;
    overview 61

habitus 32–33, 34
higher education: as field of play
    33–34; participation in 3, 11,
    19, 66; stratification of 10–11;
    transformation of 10; universities as
    agents within 49; in US 15; *see also*
    doing higher education differently
Higher Education Academy (HEA) 9

identification and belonging 37
institutional habitus 12, 50, 69

loans for part-time students 22
local, staying, for university 19, 21

map, as metaphor 1–2
mapping, as research tool 50–52
Mapping Belonging activity:
    Metropolitan Elite University 75–76;
    Modern Eastern University 75; New
    Ecclesiastical University 73–74;
    Northern City University 74–75;
    overview 51–52, 73
Massey, Doreen 28, 39–42, 47, 49, 57
Mercator Projection 2
Metropolitan Elite University:
    belonging in higher education at 68;
    dimensions of belonging at 78–79;
    doing higher education differently
    at 72–73; geographies of power at
    64–65; mapping belonging at 75–76;
    overview 53–54; scene setting for
    60–61
Modern Eastern University: belonging
    in higher education at 67; dimensions
    of belonging at 78; doing higher
    education differently at 71–72;

geographies of power at 64; mapping
    belonging at 75; overview 53; scene
    setting for 59–60
multiple case study method 48–49

New Ecclesiastical University: belonging
    in higher education at 65–66;
    dimensions of belonging at 76–77;
    doing higher education differently
    at 69–70; geographies of power at
    61–63; mapping belonging at 73–74;
    overview 53; scene setting for 58
Northern City University: belonging
    in higher education at 66–67;
    dimensions of belonging at 77–78;
    doing higher education differently
    at 70–71; geographies of power at
    63; mapping belonging at 74–75;
    overview 53; scene setting for 59

Open University 21, 22

Paired Peers study 34
participation in higher education 3, 11,
    19, 66
participatory diagramming 51
partnering contradictory perspectives 27
part-time students: challenges for
    21–23; cohorts of 68, 76, 78, 82–83;
    demographics of 19–20; Facebook
    groups for 70; identity of 37; at New
    Ecclesiastical University 62–63;
    at Northern City University 63; as
    pushed to periphery 81–82; Robbins
    Report and 20–21; as starting ahead
    of Freshers Week 73; visibility of 21
Paul Hamlyn Foundation 9
pen portraits 53–54
personal tutoring system 71–72
polytechnics 10
post-1992 universities 3, 10–11, 12, 34
power: regimes of, within higher
    education 36–37; space as product
    of social relations shaped by 40;
    see also geographies of power
practice, belonging in higher education
    as 35
pre-1992 universities 10–11, 12

queer theory 27

relational, belonging as 3, 31–36
retention *see* student retention
Robbins Committee on Higher
    Education report 10, 20–21
Robbins Principle 10

scene setting: Metropolitan Elite
    University 60–61; Modern Eastern
    University 59–60; New Ecclesiastical
    University 58; Northern City
    University 59; overview 57–58
'serious fictions' 2, 52
social, belonging as 3, 36–38
Solnit, Rebecca 51
spatial thinking 39–42, 47–48, 49
student belonging *see* belonging in
    higher education
student development theory 25–26
student retention: defined 9;
    Metropolitan Elite University 68;
    New Ecclesiastical University

65–66; part-time students and
    21; sense of belonging and 5, 9;
    significance of 11–12; studies of 11;
    see also What Works? programme
students *see* part-time students
student withdrawal or departure: post-
    1992 universities and 12; research
    into 11; Tinto's model of 13–16; in
    US 15

thinking spatially 39–42, 47–48, 49
Tinto's model of student departure
    13–16

university, as activity space 41–42

What Works? programme 5, 9, 12–13
widening participation in higher
    education 3, 11, 66
withdrawal *see* student withdrawal or
    departure

Printed in the United States
by Baker & Taylor Publisher Services